The
New Atheists

THE
NEW ATHEISTS

An Eastern Orthodox Critique

Fr. Michael Azkoul

The New Atheists
Copyright © 2020 by Fr. Michael Azkoul. All rights reserved.

No part of this publication may be reproduced, stored in a retrieval system or transmitted in any way by any means, electronic, mechanical, photocopy, recording or otherwise without the prior permission of the author except as provided by USA copyright law.

The opinions expressed by the author are not necessarily those of URLink Print and Media.

1603 Capitol Ave., Suite 310 Cheyenne, Wyoming USA 82001
1-888-980-6523 | admin@urlinkpublishing.com

URLink Print and Media is committed to excellence in the publishing industry.

Book design copyright © 2020 by URLink Print and Media. All rights reserved.

Published in the United States of America
ISBN 978-1-64753-266-6 (Paperback)
ISBN 978-1-64753-267-3 (Digital)
15.04.20

Contents

Preface..7

Chapter 1: Christ And The New Age 17

Chapter 2: The New Atheists 43

Chapter 3: The New Atheists And The True God 64

              Appendix...92

Chapter 4: New Atheism And The Church 97

Chapter 5: The Quest 134

Chapter 6: Conclusion 138

Bibliography..147

PREFACE

*The fool hath said in his heart,
There is no God.*
—Psalm 14:1

1.

This commentary is not an impartial work on atheism. The words "analysis" or "critique" or "evidence" will not be used as exclusively scientific terms. Atheism ("a-theism") under investigation is a phenomenon, peculiar to the mentality of the West, which gradually developed after its separation from the church in the East. The latter produced a culture, "Byzantine culture," which rested on the Scriptures as well as the Hellenism of the Church Fathers, Latin and Greek. The Scholastic West forged a synthesis of Christianity and Aristotle, a scheme anticipated if not initiated by Augustine of Hippo, and consummated in the *summae* of Thomas Aquinas. Their aspiration was to elevate "faith" into rational knowledge (*fides quaerens intellectum*), an enterprise that would eventually validate "the autonomy of reason," or so it was believed.

By virtue of that synthesis, the evolution (secularization) of Western philosophy, atheism was inevitable. Wrestling over the concept of God, no longer the God of the Latin and Greek Fathers, the Schoolmen fashioned a philosophical deity or being (*ens*), a concept nuanced by the Scholastics fabricating the *deus* of Aquinas and Meister Eckhart, of the Renaissance of Pompanazzi and Ficino, of the Reformation of Luther and Jonathan Edwards, of the Enlightenment of Hume and Kant, and of the Romanticism of Hegel and Schleiermacher. From these came the nineteenth-century scientism of Darwin and Marx, the psychology of Nietzsche and Freud, and the most prolific era of atheism. More profound in every way, these were the predecessor to our Four Horsemen (Dawkins, Hitchens, Harris, and Dennett). Atheism had been an elitist virus until the "evangelizing" New Atheists induced a plague for the masses.

A late convert to Deism ("the world's most notorious atheist"), Antony Flew (1923–2010) excoriated them for not presenting "a plausible world view that accounts for the existence of a 'law abiding,' 'life-supporting' and rationally accessible universe, their thinking muddled by the ups and downs of positivism." Ignoring Flew's counsel, the New Atheists have placed their trust in evolution as well as cultural Marxism and social Darwinism, which they are certain will finally supply the answers to all the great ethical questions that have tormented the human race from its beginning, a tribulation that the New Atheists assigned to religion.

There is no more vituperative enemy of Christian theism than the biologist Richard Dawkins, who prefers anecdote to "evidence," "selective internet trawling for quotes which displace rigorous and comprehensive engagement with primary sources" (A/J McGrath). He goes so far as to examine the traditional arguments for the existence of God but is "clearly out of his depth" when disparaging this weighty philosophical speculation. He displays, for example, no evidence of having read Anselm and Aquinas dispassionately, if at all. He knows nothing of the complexity of epistemological problems with all their philosophical, political and ethical, social, and economic ramifications. The writings of Dawkins give no evidence of his having read Kant, whose theology may be compared with the medieval Guanilo's rejection of Anselm's ontological argument. Among the Four Horsemen, he is not alone in unfairly deprecating what he has failed to honestly examine, such as Pascal's wager. Incidentally, his supercilious *The God Delusion* was fiercely excoriated by many of his peers.

Christopher Hitchens follows Dawkins in his abomination of God and religion albeit the former is more droll and glib. He is equally as ignorant of Christianity as Dawkins, etc. As most atheists, he is no partisan of logic. They are all inflexible materialists and monists, metaphysical theories that have been contested by philosophers time and time again, if not by the poets and novelists and, to be sure, theologians. David Bentley Hart has denounced Hitchens's faith as "equally doctrinaire secularist," which is, even now "the least attentive among us who have noticed, a historical tradition so steeped in blood that it can hardly be said to have proved its ethical superiority." When confronted by the deeds of the most infamous atheists of the twentieth century—Stalin, Mao, Pol Pot, Hitler, Castro, and others "not so great"—it never occurred to him that all religions are not the same; all religions are not good; and for example, Hitler's *Gott* is not the biblical God. Hitchens ought to know better. The God of Christianity is the Holy Trinity, a fact generally ignored in all those tiresome debates before college students, whose existence is the only one that should be under discussion.

2.

Most people interested in such things generally agree that the New Atheist movement began with the attack upon New York's Twin Towers in 2001. Led by such luminaries, such as Richard Dawkins, Sam Harris, Daniel Dennett, and the late Christopher Hitchens, they were inspired by the current secular zeitgeist, which included a vigorous opposition to religious fundamentalism. In fact, they were opposed to all supernatural religions, whatever their social value, without the idea of God. "The fact that it gives life meaning, that it makes people feel good is not an argument for the truth of religious doctrine. Furthermore, it is no argument that it is reasonable to believe that Jesus really was born of a virgin or that the Bible is the perfect word of the creator of the universe." They likewise trash the Old Testament with the same vigor that they treated the New Testament. An important addendum is that among their ranks, especially Harris, Dawkins, Dennett, and Hitchens, cannot read Hebrew, Latin, or Greek.

As many have observed, "the Four Horsemen" display an abysmal ignorance of almost every topic they address, including the Scriptures. Materialist, hiding behind a clutter of antireligious sentiments. The benefits of religion have indeed brought wonder and beauty and consolation and heroism, something that Harris and his associates will not concede. Moreover, they have not the slightest notion about the concept of sanctity. Perhaps they should have given some of their time to reading works, such Rudolf Otto's *The Idea of the Holy*, which might help revise their understanding of religion. Harris, etc., may come to view religion and "the Holy" as more than a "state of mind" and more than "neural" phenomena, that is, excitable cells that process and transmit information through chemical signals. Perhaps then the idea of the human soul might appear more than tentative.

Daniel C. Dennett, the philosopher who teaches at Tufts University, is perhaps best known as a cognitive scientist, that is, "computationalism" or that human thinking is a form of computing. Yet in his books, he offers no proficient display of philosophy. I have yet to see an analysis of Descartes, Spinoza, Locke, Kant, Hegel, etc., and their relation to his understanding to the conceptual foundations of evolutionary biology without calling for the extinction of religion. In his *Darwin's Dangerous Idea*, he argued that evolution extends far beyond biology. It has reached out to reconceptualize culture and science itself. "The Darwinian revolution," he argues, "is both a scientific and philosophical revolution, and neither could have occurred without the other."

Dennett's denial of the existence of God begins with his rebuttal of "natural theology" (i.e., the knowledge of God from nature) for which he, not unlike the other New Atheists, invokes David Hume, his *Dialogues Concerning Natural Religion*, where he states that any attempt to prove the existence of God must end in disillusionment. He was unwilling to concede to God any rational bearing upon the destiny of man or that belief in him has any relevance to the conduct of human life. Hume, like the New Atheists, did not take the time to philosophically justify the materialism (empiricism) that their opinions presuppose. Of course, many of them simply hate philosophy. Massimo Pigliuchi refers to many of them as bores if for no other reason than their philosophy brings them problems the New Atheists cannot or are unwilling to resolve.

To be sure, they appeal to David Hume, but he is really no ally despite his rejection of miracles and arguments for the existence of God. He is not their ally if only because he is not an atheist. Also, my suspicion is that while he was in their camp, the late Antony Flew may have given them guidance if not example. It was he who said, "To believe there is a God, we must have good grounds for the belief. But if no such grounds are provided, there exists no sufficient reason for believing in God, and the only reasonable position is to be a negative atheist or an agnostic (by negative I mean 'a-theist,' parallel to such words as atypical or amoral)." What is more, "the onus of proof must lie with the theists." He contended eventually that the evidence, drawn from the DNA, was sufficient to substantiate his conversion to Deism.

Despite the validity of their arguments (now strengthened by Flew's action), the opponents of the New Atheists are yet expected to surrender their agenda to them. Not only is New Atheist's undeclared philosophy burdened with all the great metaphysical and epistemological questions asked throughout the intellectual history of the West, but their arguments are also impeded by their visceral and almost hysterical opposition to theism. If there is any opposition between religion and science, it is they who erect it. In truth, there never has been any contradiction between them so long as each remained within the arena of their competence, that is, science confining its queries to the natural world, while religion dealing with matters of transcendence, the realm of the spirit. Hence, it is not the business of science to prove or disprove the existence of God. Nevertheless, as the history of science itself has shown, science has always naturally assumed the existence of a supernatural designer. Religion need not meddle in matters concerning the electromagnetic field or the nature of energy, save that God is the author and designer of the cosmos.

Watching the debates between the atheists and the theist, which are usually parallel speeches rather than *aller et retour* disputes, one is often astonished to observe the latter to be disarmed or intimidated by his antagonist. The theist compulsively retreats to the traditional arguments for the existence of God and is put on the defensive when charges hurled against religion (e.g., the Inquisition, the Crusades). Also, they are often caught off balance when Dawkins or Hitchens mock their creeds as full of contradictions, superstitions, and legends and that the God of the Old Testament is not "a moral monster," for instance, in the "mythical tale of Noah and the Flood," where he saved eight people and destroyed the world, along with the "innocent children and animals." Likewise, in the New Testament God the Father kills his own Son for the sins of others, the human race, which inherited the guilt of Adam and Eve. It seems never to have occurred to Christian theists that there might be another explanation for the atonement, that is, Christ died on the Cross to destroy the power of death. In the language of the Paschal Troparion (fifth tone), "Christ is risen from the dead, having conquered death by death and on the dead bestowing life." The error of the New Atheists is the result of their presupposing in their criticism an erroneous occidental Christology.

In other words, if the arguments of Christian apologists (most notably John Lennox, professor of mathematics at Oxford, and William Lane Craig, professor of philosophy at Biola University) have no effect on the dedicated atheist, it is not only because of the conflicts of faiths but also strangely because they initiate their clash with the same religio-philosophical categories. The New Atheists are not being persuaded that we can leap from physics and biology to the existence of a personal God. Also, the theists have hoped also to confute atheists with an appeal to religious experience, even philosophy, when they might have taken the offensive with a charge against the New Atheists spiritual condition, an impediment that blocks their access to spiritual truth to which the human being has access only by piety and divine enlightenment. Finally, there is nothing compelling in the answer "No one. He is eternal" to the infantile question "Who made God?" Reason alone cannot change the heart.

In other words, the right tactic is to avoid confronting the New Atheists on their own level. At best, only a stalemate has been achieved. To be sure, the atheist cannot prove that the universe has no spiritual dimension, but the theist by mere logic cannot demonstrate it does. The New Atheists seem to hold the field despite their often clumsy and erroneous arguments, holding it because the conventional Christian and theist apologist fears his religious stance prejudices his case, while any accusation of sinfulness against atheist gives the appearance of "holier than thou" with no help from the hypocrisy of so many believers.

In any case, the God defended and denied is unaware to them an idol, an abstraction, a philosophical God as cause, as object, an analogy to our created being, albeit, to be sure, supremely perfect. But the true God must be sought outside the realm of the Western philosophical and theological tradition, which has blinded them to the truth. There is another religious vision that places "the one true God" beyond all rational knowledge, beyond the ken of human rationality, beyond being (*hyperousios*), the "knowledge" of that God and the worldview that surrounds him offer a unique perspective on all the questions raised, all the conclusions drawn concerning him and his relation to his creation. It is the purpose of this book to show that the debate between the occidental theist and atheists is futile because it rests on false premises.

We cannot hope to provide in the few pages of this paper "the holy grail," but perhaps we can open new avenues of thought. Yes, there can be comments on the moral and intellectual foibles of the Four Horsemen but not by the same jejune weapons commonly launched against them—*argumenta existentia Dei* by Aristotle, Anselm, Aquinas, Pascal, and Voltaire—not even Dostoyevsky's "If there is no God, everything is permitted." They are ready with retorts to these theories. The New Atheists live by a faith with far less credence than those whom they accuse of living by fanciful dreams and "wishful thinking." Of course, the faith of the one is the **self**, the point at which they are most vulnerable, and of other, the faith in a loving God. In a sense, the weakness of the one is matched by the other: a deity about whom they are both wrong and for which reason their struggle is meaningless.

It is therefore necessary to distinguish between Christianity and all other religions lest the distinction between them becomes futile. Then, too, the claims of Christianity must be disregarded. She must cling to the axiom that is true is "All religions may be false, only one may be true." For this reason also, St. Paul declared, "Endeavoring to keep the unity of the Spirit in the bond of peace, There is one body, one Spirit, even as you are called in one hope of your calling: one Lord, one faith, one baptism, one God and Father of all who is above all, and through all, and in you all" (Eph. 4:3–6). This is the complement to the words of St. John the Evangelist, "And this is eternal life that they might know the one true God and Jesus Christ Whom He has sent" (Jn. 17:3). The claim of Christianity is that truth and salvation are revealed, not discovered. To be sure, she has a physical and institutional dimension, a "phenomenon" as Dennett insists, but is she essentially divine even as Christ is the unity of the human and the divine without "separation or confusion"?

This is the essence of Christian exclusivism, which to the mind of many is more than intolerance. The validity of reason's conclusions rests on the "evidence" that is rising from the sense-data. In any dispute then between atheists and theists, the "onus of proof" falls on both sides if for no other reason than that there is more than one kind of "proof" or "evidence" for the existence of anything. The so-called autonomous reason has seen to that. Once the New Atheists come to grips with this fact, they will need to reconsider the conditions of the debate.

The art of the syllogism offers nothing so long as the major premise is indemonstrable. Dialectic is not "the sword of truth" unless it corresponds with reality. Perhaps if they made the acquaintance of the themes and spirit of the theology of the Church Fathers—without the computer, the ancient documents, or even the usual patrologies of Tixeront, Quasten, Bardenhewer, etc.—the New Atheists might be intrigued by something familiar on the surface but so radically different in its core and that despite the patristic ardor for the "supernatural." They will be introduced to images, concepts, and principles beyond the deprecated "medieval" or "sectarian" venues of thought. They might see Christianity in another light. If so, then the New Atheism must be reconstructed or rejected completely.

If the reader can at least suspend his investment in all the Western religious and philosophical shibboleths, which now persuade him; if he/she will ignore the latest developments in "religion"; if he/she will dispose of the unprofitable assumption that church history must be viewed as words, ideas, and doctrines in process; and if he/she will show a healthy skepticism toward the contemporary histories of Christianity and withhold his vexation toward the "scandals" in religions, theism in particular produces a spark of curiosity which may earn him a new reward, which the pretensions of the Four Horsemen cannot provide, especially if we consider that incompetent theologians, inept historians, and bungling philosophers now plague our minds. Integrity is not their strength.

If nothing else, our expostulations may introduce the New Atheists and others like them to something strange, something to which they have not given any thought, a world of deliberation and activity caught up in the agony of theoretical *uncertainty*, a storm of and the abyss of relativism. Some of what is said here may be offensive to those, even proud theist, with another mind-set, punctuating their protestation with the exclamation, "that's something you cannot expect us to believe." But here is a challenge to secular modernity and to its representatives, the New Atheists.

Let it be understood that atheism is not merely an opponent of religion; it is a substitute for it. Man has replaced God, that is to say, worship never ceases as Feuerbach tells us. There is God, the devil, and the flesh. The latter two have the same consequences. Man, in disdaining his own littleness and aspiring to the divine majesty, gains no virtue or moral perfection but rather is trapped in the devil's net. Death is rampant; sin is afire. George Bernard Shaw was wrong; it is not without reason that we blunder into death but rather without the soteric faith, the faith revealed in the God-man, he that by his redemption would transform mortal man into god by participation in things. Is that not after all what the New Atheists really want, divinity? Was not Shestov right when he said the selfish desire of

Adam and Eve was to *know* good and evil to be as God, which, ironically, deprived them of what God had planned as their destiny?

Put another way, the conquest of atheism and its cry for absolute and universal secularism is only possible with a radically new worldview. My recommendation is the "philosophy" of the Church Fathers for so long disdained and therefore marginalized, no, so long trivialized in the modern West. For too long, they have been treated as an obsolete stage in the development of the Christian religion. To be sure, this is a beginning. But it is not sufficient in the struggle against secularization and the atheism to simply oppose them with religious fervor. At the heart of the problem in our decadent occidental culture is the theory of knowledge, epistemology, thanks to Descartes and Kant. So long as the "problem" goes unresolved, nothing is safe from this tarantula, the worldview that gave life to the New Atheists, to all atheists. It will continue to breed.

Fr. Michael Azkoul

CHAPTER I

CHRIST AND THE NEW AGE

Glory to man in the highest!
For man is the master of all things!
—A. C. Swinburne

A. N. Wilson observed Dostoyevsky's lament that nineteenth-century Europe had lost, by virtue of its growing atheism, a sense of the transcendent, the sublime and therefore of human purpose. It was a sickness "which subsequently infected Russia as a result of the espousal of Western rationalism and materialism."[1] His conclusion was not a wild suspicion that the nineteenth-century "experiment" was an attempt by European intellectuals to renounce Christ and to live without the Creator. Darwinism is a clear account of his fears. Although he might have supposed it, he did not know that the secularism that had invaded his country would lead to regicide of God's anointed to the assassination of Tsar Nicholas II and to the close of "the Constantinian era" while obviating the medieval Christian synthesis, which had been so forcefully articulated in the of Thomas Aquinas. The result of pursuing a reconstitution of Western culture on radically secular and non-Christian grounds raised once more those terrifying questions about the nature of reality and the destiny of man.

It was the revival of atheism that generated a "transvaluation of values" nowhere better expressed than the French Revolution ("atheism in the streets") and the philosophical atheism of the German universities with its new weltanschauung of the materialism and positivism and pantheism of Romantic idealism, all inhaled by the so-called Enlightenment of the previous century that, under the auspices of Scottish philosopher David Hume, removed "any philosophical necessity for believing in the Christian God."2 The nineteenth-century philosophers concerned themselves with question of whether traditional religion had any meaning for human life and thought. Unlike the thinkers of the previous century who asked whether there is a first cause of things, the twentieth century has replied in the negative, largely on account of the ostensible omnicompetent physical sciences, not the least of which was the theory of evolution. Inasmuch as "God is dead!" there was nothing left but the genius of man. The New Atheists or Four Horsemen have claimed the role of its contemporary prophets.

There was nothing more important to the development of modern philosophy, and indirectly to the physical sciences, than the work of Immanuel Kant (1724–1804), who himself had launched the nineteenth century with an attempt to reconcile the two competing philosophical forces that had addicted Europe from the time of Descartes: empiricism and idealism (both of which may be called rationalism). He was awakened from his "dogmatic slumbers" by Hume, who had questioned, on strictly empirical grounds, the possibility of epistemic "predictability" and "causality," a doubt that if true, would surely demolish the aspirations of physical sciences. Hume had set thought (subject) against being (object), an epistemological duality that, according to his treatment of them, would leave the quest for theoretical certainty futile and, at the same time, would place the concepts as God, immortality, and free will beyond the competence of reason (*Vernunft*) to fruitfully examine.

Kant did not abandon the duality of thought (subject) and being (object). He reworked it metaphysically. For Kant, "human reason is ineradicably metaphysical," says N. K. Smith. "He took the path of inner experience and evident consciousness." Until his time, it was assumed by philosophers that that human thinking must adjust to the object it confronted. He, therefore, posited that objects; or the world of the senses should conform to reason, that is, the "manifold of senses" or sense impressions or phenomena coming to the mind to be organized (including predictability and causality). Yet reason is unable to find the source of the knowable, visible, developing phenomena, the unknowable, imperceptible, unchangeable reality that Kant called noumenon or thing-in-itself (*das-an-sich*). In other words, he hoped to resolve the problem raised by empiricism with a metaphysic of the self.

Kant's new metaphysics or "critical philosophy" was grounded in the experience (*empirisch*) of the self or the duality of phenomena and noumenon or, in the words of Lev Shestov, "the postulate beyond which we cannot go."[3] But not everyone agreed with his solution. They saw in his *Critique of Pure Reason* a glossing over of the ontological fissure his work had opened. His disciple, Johann Gottlieb Fichte (1762–1814), saw no reason to bifurcate mysterious noumenon and world of phenomena. The former cannot be unknowable, or else we would not recognize that it was. To know that it exists is, in fact, to go beyond the noumenon. Something unknowable cannot be known to exist. In other words, there is no philosophy, save idealism with its a priori method; and reason does not discover the truth but produces it. Outside the pure good or moral ego, designated by many "the absolute" or "Spirit," there is nothing but the self or "ego and the nonego" (nature) that unite to create the truth, that is, the objective world. To be sure, Fichte admitted with Kant that the thing-in-itself cannot be reduced to thought; nevertheless, the duality of thought and being is ultimately a chimera.

From Kant and Fichte, George Hegel (1770–1831) took his *point de depart*. What Kant called God and Fichte the good, Hegel designated the absolute mind or Spirit. It passes through the states of development in time and becomes conscious of itself in the human reason—the self. It incarnates itself in time, space, and humanity. It is history or, to be more precise, the Spirit unfolds dialectically *with* the cosmos. Put another way, the first principle of thought is being (thesis). It is negated by its opposite, nonbeing (antithesis). They are united in becoming (synthesis). History is nothing more than becoming or "progress" (*werden*), that is, dialectic or unfolding and merging opposites. This "becoming" of the universe (of the Spirit) manifests that "God" is immanent, that it is all. Until the nineteenth century, the West had generally accepted the "classical consciousness" or linear, unrepeatable, and intelligible events; but with Hegel, Europe had gained a "historical consciousness." There is no transcendence, no supernatural, merely history or the sequence of events within time-space. History will answer our questions even as "the Christian God" might have. He had been conceived as the Redeemer, while Hegel's deity is essentially a process of self-alienation (as the other from being) that returns to itself (synthesis)—a circle, the going out and return to itself. A very Greek conception: cyclicism: the beginning and the end are the same. This is Hegel's major postulate out of which his disciples each will construct his own worldview.

Some attention must be given to the Christology of this period inasmuch as the identity of Christ is a necessary component in identifying the biblical God. The unholy triad of Kant, Fichte, and Hegel is not without relevance in this matter. Today there is no necessary connection among God, Christ, and the Trinity. If Christ is God, the Son of the only true God, there is obviously no atheism unless God is the Trinity; and it is he who is denied or redefined. In other words, there can be no understanding of the nineteenth-century reconceptions of God without the rejection of the "biblical Jesus" or "historical Jesus." Here is a Christology that owes its major premises to Hegel. If nothing else, Hegel reinterpreted Christ for his own generation and, yes, the future, for none of these philosophers is he the transcendent God-man but the symbol of the immanent humanization or an unfolding spiritual dimension of reality, "God-manhood" whose consummate realization is the personality of Jesus Christ.[4] To be deified is the goal of every human being. It is a Christological "truth" that complements the entire cosmogonic-cosmological process.

THE NEW ATHEISTS

Of course, it is Hegel who gave legitimacy to the idea of the sovereignty of the earth's new ruler. His Left Hegelians disciples5 brought it to celebrity in the social and intellectual convulsions of the nineteenth century, none with such self-conscious vigor as David Strauss (1808–1874). While a student at Tuebingen, he was swept along by the Romantic movement. There, he became acquainted with the writings of Jakob Boehme (1575–1624), whom Hegel called "the father of German philosophy." Like the other devotees of the movement, Strauss was in search of the supernatural. Tackling the question of faith and reason, he came to the conclusion that Hegel was wrong to identify theology and philosophy, the human and the divine. Thus, he insisted that the two realities were opposed.[6] Strauss's Christology came to maturity under the influence of Ferdinand Baur (1792–1860), who raised his interest in the Bible as a philosophical source. None confirmed his embrace of idealism more than the system of Friedrich Schelling (1775–1854), who declared that "history as a whole is a continuous, gradually self-disclosing revelation of the Absolute." Positing this historiosophy, "the Christ-event" becomes merely the locus at which the theological process is maximized. He is not, as the Savior is with the Fathers of the Church, the image of history; or rather, as Schweitzer thought, the concept of history depends upon one's concept of Christ.

In fact, the existence of Christ is the "event" when God and man are essentially identical because human history is the level of existence at which the divine is revealed (*Offenbarung*). Here also, the religious interest in Christ becomes indistinguishable from the philosophical interest. In other words, what Strauss learned from Baur was a predilection for treating theological issues as philosophy, that is, a way of showing how the estrangement of God from the world is overcome. Next, Baur introduced Strauss to the works of Friedrich Schleiermacher (1768–1834), the grand progenitor of liberal Protestantism. Perhaps under his influence, Strauss came to believe that it was impossible to draw an authentic picture of a historical Jesus if he continued to think of him as transcendentally divine. If he did anything for him, Schleiermacher corroborated Strauss's vision of history's goal as the reconciliation of the divine and the human, the infinite and finite, whose end is "the restoration of all things" (*apokatastasis ton panton*), a theory well known to the ancient Greeks.

Such was the theme of Strauss's famous *The Life of Jesus*, one of many books by that title in the nineteenth century. He postulated that the Incarnation encompassed humanity as a whole, not a single historical figure. It was clear to him that the historicity of the "Christ-event" was no longer tenable if it was conceived as transcendent. Any such notion was rejected inasmuch as the absolute was everywhere immanent; in a word, there is nothing supernatural. Traditional Christianity was no longer a viable choice precisely because the idea of transcendence or the supernatural is obsolete. The medieval dualism of nature and grace had been replaced by idealist monism. Necessarily then, the doctrine of Christ as Redeemer rests on the false notions of a supernatural God become man. Thus, the Christian doctrine of the Incarnation, Crucifixion, and the Resurrection is the folly of hallucinated zealots. Naturally, Strauss found no more interest in the Gospels as icons of Christ's miraculous life.

Necessarily, the Hegelian metaphysic begot the Christology of Strauss and company, which begot a new study of the Scriptures; and from this *Kulturkampf* between Western Christianity and secular modernity arose the "higher criticism" of the Bible. No name is so preeminent in this aspect of the controversy than Julius Wellhausen (1844–1918). His specialty was the Old Testament (OT). Of course, he was intimidated by Hegel but also drew intellectual sustenance from Goethe and Darwin. Without a personal God, there was no place for revelation, and there was no such thing as inerrant Scriptures. The OT was ranked with the other sacred books of the ancients, which made similar claims to inspiration and revelation. Subjected to the historical and philological analysis, the literary texts could not produce the narrative intended by its authors; instead, the "higher criticism" of Wellhausen and his associates elicited a history of Israel as a perfect example of the universal evolution of all religions from animism to monotheism. Of course, Jehovah was a tribal deity. It was the prophets who were the true religious innovators and who produced most, if not all, of what became distinctive of Israel, the grand culmination of its thought coming with the universalism of sixth century BC Second Isaiah (chapters 40–55). To fit this theory, the Scriptures were necessarily reworked over time to fit the evidence as the higher critics saw it.

In any case, the reduction of the Scriptures to "great religious literature" secured the way for nineteenth-century atheism and "the revaluation of values." These creators of a new "world order" did not need to look back— no miracles, no authority, no judgment, no reward, and no punishment.

The Young Hegelians of the Left were profoundly impressed by Strauss's Christology, especially Ludwig Feuerbach (1804–1882), whose work, incidentally, was a fundamental principle of Marxian socialism. He adapted the Hegelian dialectic with a single but crucial difference; it was not the absolute (God) that was "alienated" and "striving" for reconciliation with itself in man. Never was that imposing idea of the nineteenth-century glorification of man more ingeniously delineated than in the philosophy of Ludwig Feuerbach. The familiar metaphor "Hegel stood on his head" is no better applied than here. The Feuerbachian "inversion" posits that man reconciles God to himself; hence, it is implied that man is "God." "If I deny God that means for me that I deny the negation of man. The existence of a personal, transcendent God implies the alienation of man from himself." In other words, the question about the existence or nonexistence of God is for Feuerbach really a question about the existence or nonexistence of man. He was certain that he could demonstrate that "religion itself says: God is man, man is God ..."[7]

According to Feuerbach, Christianity with its doctrine of the Incarnation has given us the truth in reverse, that is, lowering God into man to elevate man into God. The "true sense" of this theology is anthropology: God is a dream of the human heart, an awareness of his authentic self, that is, the Christian religion is "God-consciousness." "Consciousness of God is self- consciousness, knowledge of God as self-knowledge."[8] Self-knowledge is the awareness of the projection of his being into objectivity. He has made himself an object to himself but as the object of an object, of a being other than himself. He himself is an object to himself. Put another way, the self mentally throws himself outward, that is, objectifying himself, worshipping the object of him. The object (which he calls *God*) is the antithesis of him. It is his ideal self that he worships. Thus, in religion, man contemplates his own latent nature. The task of the individual is to identify the self with the "ideal image" of himself. The self and the object, the projected self will realize the truth only when they are reunited as a synthesis.

The "task of the modern era" is the conversion of theology into anthropology. It was at the end of his Heidelberg lectures that Feuerbach indicated his principal aim: "to change the friends of God into the friends of man, believers into thinkers, worshippers into workers, candidates for the world to students to the world, Christians, who on their own confessions are half-animal, half-angel, into men—whole men." Consequently, as Marx said, "theologians must become anthropologians … religious and political footmen of a celestial and terrestrial monarchy and transforming aristocracy into free, self-reliant citizens of earth."[9] Here is the "inversion" of Christianity: the metamorphosis of God into earthly man, man dedicated to the perfection of the earth.

Moreover, the Incarnation of Jesus Christ reveals the truth of "humanization of God." We can ignore the biblical Christ, the Christ of the Fathers (about which he knew very little unless we count Augustine among them). "The Incarnation is nothing else than the practical, material manifestation of the human nature of God. God did not become man for his own sake; the need, the want of man—a want which still exists in the religious sentiment—was the cause of the Incarnation," Feuerbach wrote in the *Essence of Christianity* (1841). "The incarnate God is only the apparent manifestation of deified man … Christ, one might say, was the human form of God."[10] Furthermore, "the mystery of the Incarnation is "the love of man for himself," that is, his "true self," his perfect self, his free and reconciled self realized finally in the everlasting union between man and his projected self. Feuerbach wants us to believe that the "alienation" or "schism" between the visible and ideal self is overcome in Christ, the one who typifies their reconciliation. He is the deified man, the beginning of man's return to himself.

But there is more to the Incarnation. It is also the "inversion" of the Trinitarian life, which is mirrored in human relationships. The Father is "I," and the Son is "Thou" even as is the case between two persons. The Holy Spirit is nothing more than the "love" between Father and Son. It is here that Feuerbach raises the idea of society or community, for the Holy Spirit is the love with which God loves himself and man; and therefore, he is the love with which men love one another. He is the "unity or identity already involved in the idea of the Father and yet more in that of the Son." Inasmuch as the Holy Spirit is "obviously the poetic personification," there is no reason to make it a separate object of analysis.[11] He is the creature sighing for God or, if we may say, the self in quest for reunion with itself. Finally, Feuerbach must add that God with which man seeks to be reconciled is not a spirit. He speaks of "the Night of God," an expression that always implies something "material, corporeal, fleshly" about him and necessarily about man himself.

There is a further suggestion in his concept of the "materiality" of God, not merely that he was incarnate and represents humanity. It does seem that he introduced a female element in God by virtue of readings in German mysticism, which is the source of "the eternal feminine" (*die ewig Weibliche*). The notion that Christ is "man" or "humanity" (*anthropos*) must necessarily include the woman, that is to say, Christ is male and female— androgynous. Since the love of the son to the mother is the first love, it follows that this love, as all love, is a metaphysical yearning; and consequently, the idea of the Mother of God is associated with the idea of the Son of God, the same heart that needs the one the other needs. Likewise, the idea of love extends to the love between a man and a woman, a love wrought by the Holy Spirit, a union analogous to the tandem of love and generation within the Trinity.

Finally, "the new philosophy" makes man the unique, universal, and highest object of philosophy and, to be sure, anthropology with the inclusion of physiology, the universal science. This atheistic humanism of Feuerbach will be essential to the Marxian anthropology. Feuerbach was concerned with man as a religious being, Marx with him as *homo economicus*. To be sure, Hegel taught him that "alienation" is the central fact of history (*entfremdungsgeschichte*), but it was from Feuerbach that the self stood at the center of the Marxian narrative. He came to understand that it was at the heart of the human condition; and of course, the solution was to be found in materialism, which is after all the basis of all existence.

Marx described himself as a "scientific socialist"; yet materialism is not a science but a metaphysic. With regard to this fact, it is important to recognize that he views history as a progressive process of purification, with perfection, in the form of socialism as its end. To go further, Marx's historiosophy is utopian and deterministic, that is to say, he prophecies the decay of capitalism and the triumph of the proletarian. Ludwig von Mises uses the word "chiliastic" because it goes beyond experience, which atheism never fails to do. Also, his chiliasm may have Judaic antecedents. Moreover, his endorsement of Darwinism impels Marx to portray materialistic historiosophy as "cosmic evolution." Also interesting is his belief that history proceeds to "paradise," to a golden age; in a word, Marxism promises an earthly salvation. If this is true, Von Mises says that it is "vain and superfluous" to argue scientifically against Marxian teleology. Finally, it is a theory of history based on the necessity of struggle, an idea for which he was thankful to Darwin for confirming "scientifically." There is an addendum (no better illustrated than the "science" of Richard Dawkins) that most atheistic biologists are "enslaved" to Marxian socialism.[12]

Marx was also validated in his collectivism by Feuerbach's "I-Thou" paradigm. To establish it, he had to deflect the attack from the philosophy of Max Stirner (1806–1856), who was an exponent of anarchic individualism expounded in his *The Ego and Its Own*. He too echoed Nietzsche's cry he should be a god. Stirner had little in common with Marxian egalitarianism and did not join him in his call for "class warfare." In his *The German Ideology*, Marx claimed to have disposed of the threat from St. Max as he called him. There, he spoke of the real man, the man no longer "alienated" by economic forces. Here too is his version of Hegel's "unity of the human and the divine" in which Marx argues that atheism is the natural concomitant to materialist historiosophy. He stressed the notion that man is the only infinite thing, the only deity. With confidence, he declared that only objects of perception are phenomenal. Lifeless matter was the rudimentary substance of reality.[13]

In part, Marxist historiosophy is the result of a critique of religion. Feuerbach convinced him that it was a serious hindrance to "genuine" metaphysics. Without its eradication, his "construction of a new way of life" would not succeed. Necessarily then, an independent and superior otherworld is inimical to his vision of man and history:

> *Man, who has found in the fantastic reality of heaven, where he sought a supernatural being, only his own reflection, will no longer be tempted to find only the semblance of himself—a non-human where he seeks and must seek his true reality. The basis of irreligious criticism is this:* man makes religion, religion does not make man. *Religion is indeed man's self-consciousness and self- awareness so long as he has not found himself or has lost him again. But man is not an abstract being, squatting outside this world. Man is the human world, the state, society. This state, this society, produces religion where is an inverted world consciousness, because they are an inverted world. Religion is the general theory of this world, it's encyclopedic compendium, its logic in popular form, its spiritual point d'honneur, its enthusiasm ... The struggle against religion is, therefore, directly a struggle against that world whose spiritual aroma is religion. Religious suffering is at the same time an expression of real suffering, a protest against real suffering. Religion is the sigh of the oppressed creature, the sentiment of a heartless world, and the soul of soulless conditions. It is the opium of the people. The abolition of religion as the illusory happiness of men, is a demand for their real happiness. The call to abandon their illusions about their condition is a call to abandon a condition which requires illusions. The criticism of religion is, therefore, the embryonic criticism of this vale of tears of which religion is the halo?*[14]

Marx believed that the immediate task of philosophy was to establish "the truth of this world: to unmask human self-alienation in its *secular form* now that it has unmasked it in its sacred form." In other words, "the criticism of heaven is transformed into the criticism of earth, the criticism of religion into the criticism of law, the criticism of theology into the criticism of politics."[15] We see that Marx argued in tones reminiscent of Feuerbach that "man is the supreme being for man." Put in other words, the sovereignty of man is "the categorical imperative" in the overthrow of all those conditions by which man is abased, enslaved, abandoned, a contemptible being—conditions in which he is treated as an animal.

If for Marx and his legion, liberation is the negation of religion, then salvation is no more than the acquisition of a new consciousness by which humanity may become "a new species of being with a new species of life." Marx insisted more strongly than Feuerbach (from whom he took these terms) that the extirpation of religion was necessary for the development of a new world. Although the task of "negating of the negation," that is, overcoming the self-alienation for which religion is largely responsible, begins now with the creation of a state, a Communist state, which features perfect equality, integration of the races and freedom through love and, to be sure, a condition of things that is antithetical to the otherworldly vision of the Christian religion.

To establish this state will not come easily. "Communist action" is initiated with the seizure of our alienated world through "revolutionary action," that is, with the eradication of "privilege" or, more specifically, of private property (*aufhebungs des privateigentums*). Private property abrogates equality and causes exploitation and bondage. Humanity will be reintegrated only with its disappearance. The change can only be accomplished by revolution, by the negation of the existing order—capitalism, in particular, which is associated with "elitist" and "aristocratic" morality of Christianity—a negation that may produce violence and death. It will bring Communism, which offers "a really human morality which overcomes the class antagonisms which separate human beings." This morality is "equality based on nature and the inalienable rights of man."[16] In other words, as atheism is the negation of God, humanism is the negation of capitalist Christian morality.

As it must be evident, the Marxian hope requires a materialistic interpretation of history. There is no "providence," only the dialectic of human events or, as Marx put it, "the algebra of revolution," a "revolution" whose aim is the overthrow of all bourgeois morality that has been hitherto the product of prevalent socioeconomic conditions. Those conditions will only vanish with the change of the morality that links humanity to the supernatural. The only constant in history is human nature in the process of modification (not without its Darwinian implications); his flight from religion and his incessant adaptation to the forces of economic production alone promise to abolish "alienated labor" in its struggle with private enterprise. Communism will come with the dawn of the final age of the world, the age of freedom, the totally naturalist, humanist, and classless society. His aspirations have not yet been entirely fulfilled, but "cultural Marxism" or "political correctness" has become the prevalent morality of the twenty-first century.

We should not be surprised that Karl Marx was enthralled when during his visit to London, he read Charles Darwin's (1809–1882) *The Origin of the Species* published in 1859. They shared the same atheism and materialism. Marx went so far as to dedicate his *Das Kapital* (1867) to the Englishman. How pleased he was that the historiosophy "he felt in his bones" was finally proven scientifically, that now everyone could see that "progress" was relentless and pitiless, mechanically determined by the laws of nature themselves. At Marx's funeral, his longtime friend and associate, Friedrich Engels (1820–1895), delivered the oration, stating that as Marx had discovered the law of development for human history, so Darwin had discovered the law of development for organic nature, while both also delivered the death blow to teleology, that is, that the historiosophical view that things have a purpose or "final end," that is, design and therefore a designer. God has been banished, no longer needed, for Darwin has provided us with the mechanism for the life of the earth, of the cosmos, the evolution of species by means of natural selection, nature's "invisible hand" in the gradual and random adaptation of species to their environment, fitting them for termination or survival. Thomas Huxley ("Darwin's bulldog") used the expression "survival of the fittest" to describe the actions of natural selection. The intellectual soil of the nineteenth century prepared the way for the appearance of Charles Darwin and the theory of biological evolution. Although he was not a philosopher, his theory (explanation) presupposed philosophical first principles—naturalism, materialism, and atheism. He was content to let others, such as Herbert Spencer (1820–1903) and Ernst Haeckel (1834–1919), draw out the philosophical implications of his biological system. "The main ideas of his theory had long been in the air: the struggle for existence, the mutability of species and natural selection, the inheritance of traits favorable to biological survival and the descent of man from a lower order of primates," observes H. D. Aiken. "It was Darwin's role to bring all these ideas together within a united hypothesis which sought to explain in terms of natural causes the development of all living things."[17] Whether Darwin hoped to build a total worldview by his writings, it is difficult to say, and it is unclear from his writings that the theory of evolution was devised to that end. Jacques Barzun does, in fact, describe it as "a complete world outlook."[18] It surely stimulated the philosophical imagination to speculate on the cosmos as a whole and on the direction it would take us.

In point of fact, Darwinian evolution is ultimately a philosophy with a frontage of science—philosophy seeking scientific verification. To repeat, it rests on a body of "first principles"—monism, materialism, and naturalism. The universe is natural with no reliance of the supernatural; it is composed of a single substance. At the same time, there is no necessary connection between these principles, that is, atheism and science. To this day, some of the world's greatest scientists confessed themselves to be Christians— Copernicus, Kepler, Galileo, Boyd, Newton, Linnaeus, Mendel, Pasteur, J. C. Maxwell, Heisenberg, Dyson, Collins, Lennox, Max Planck, the founder of quantum mechanics, etc. They are not among those who believe that divine intervention negates science. God works in his own mysterious ways to ensure the intelligibility of physical and spiritual natures. That he has designed a specie does not prevent human reason from discovering its details and purpose. If I have not misread them, the New Atheists are overjoyed that evolution has replaced the Creator with nature. It is not logic that causes them to prefer this absurdly inadequate mechanism to explain the existence of the conscious, reflecting, mathematical, mystical, poetic mind. Also, the indifference to the paranormal is arbitrary. There is nothing reliable in an instrumentality whose nature and force depend on dead matter and capricious energy, along with natural laws that may eventually change and alter the entire trajectory of our thinking.

Whether admitted, evolution's natural selection is a God-surrogate. In point of fact, there is no reason to believe that the universe was formed by this mechanistic process. With the appearance of "the big bang theory," something unknown to Darwin and unwanted by many of his disciples, the idea that the cosmos emerged from a signature moment is a threat to evolution.[19] There is no reason to believe that the universe had a beginning (unappealing to those who suspect that the big bang comes perilously close to the idea of a Creator). This cosmogony introduces to science and philosophy a number of questions that cannot be convincingly answered. There is too much speculation here. In a world with so many species adorned with so much complexity (DNA) under a variety of random mutations, an ambiguous fossil record, there is not enough time, according to numerous mathematicians concerned with the subject, to account for man and his environment. In addition, Darwin himself confessed there are numerous agents of change.

There may be something to the accusation that Darwin turned away from God when he tragically lost his young daughter. But then he had nothing left but his fame. It was a theory that rendered the God he resented unnecessary. Darwin was pleased to announce that the Genesis account of creation was no longer credible. He may not have been aware (or cared) that evolution hypothesis used nonscientific arguments to make its case. Was he cognizant that he, as so many of like disposition, was not letting the evidence lead him where he must go and his doctrine possessed unspoken premises about the nature of God and how he must have created the world? Darwin did not know that his idea of God was inherited from an intellectual tradition that ab initio espoused a notion of deity *qua* being. As C. G. Hunter surmises, "One cannot find evidence against the Divine without first assuming something about the Divine."[20] No matter; he was persuaded that evolution offers the only realistic explanation for the existence of everything. The father of positivism, Auguste Comte (1789–1857), linked his atheism with a historiosophy in which the era of science had superseded the eras of theology and philosophy. He did not need God, neither did Darwin. Whatever the truth, both fervently wanted to erase the Genesis narrative.

Denying that man was made in the "image and likeness" of the Creator, Darwin yet designated him the crown of creation by virtue of his reason. Richard Dawkins, his most dedicated acolyte, considers the human being as little more than a mix of chemistry and molecules. In opposition to his friend and colleague, Alfred Russell Wallace (1823–1913) proclaimed that natural selection made nonsense of the biblical anthropology according to which man was a "unique creature" and that his origin and destiny was a matter of concern to the "supernatural power." The eventual publication of his theory shook the scientific world and the general public, for it not only challenged the prevalent and accepted notion of natural theology (the knowledge of God from cosmic design), but it also more than implied that man's ancestry was the ape. In fact, Darwin did not insist that all life came from a simple cell, an affirmation he makes without any provision for its environment, or how the cell "happened" to extricate itself from the "primordial soup." From where did the energy come to induce its liberty? It would seem that Darwin, having no idea of the DNA (deoxyribonucleic acid), had no reason to believe otherwise, especially since he did not acknowledge the existence of a spiritual world, neither did he take the time to justify the idea that man emerged from "slime."

Necessarily, in his catalogue of beliefs, there was no room for Jesus Christ, a fortiori as the incarnate Lord and the Church, his body, which embraced two lives, one in time, the other in eternity, a dichotomy no materialism may tolerate. He was the Creator of the heavens and the earth, the God of Genesis and the Old Testament. Obviously, any concession to traditional theology and cosmogony would negate vision of things, especially the idea of creation ex nihilo in six days; however, those days or "ages" were defined. Furthermore, Darwin espoused a very old earth, perhaps five million years, even though the age of the universe reaches back twice that time. The book of Moses gives no such measure. Having abandoned Christ as Savior, he had no reason to accept the testimony of the Old Testament or the Gospels. Of the nineteenth-century thinkers, he was not the only one to reject miracles. The more we know about the fixed laws of nature, he said, the more incredible do miracles become; and with regard to the Gospel writers, he averred that they were ignorant and credulous men to "a degree almost incomprehensible to us." Summing up his opinions on the New Testament, he wrote that assessing the outrageous claims made for Christ, he came to disbelieve in Christianity as a divine revelation. Darwin was forty years old when he confessed his skepticism. Some have noted that his loss of faith in Christ and Christianity occurred before he composed his *Origin of the Species* and *The Descent of Man*, not on account of them.

There is something else that Darwin and his followers failed to consider, that is, other than his metaphysics. It holds that subject to mechanistic laws deprives man and nature of spontaneity or, if as some might say, creativity as Henri Bergson once remarked. It is generally true that Darwinists do not pay much attention to the real possibility that as human nature evolves, so does its thinking, its conceptualization. There may be also the truth that evolution acceleration varies from time to time; and yes, time itself changes, something Einstein and quantum mechanics imply. There is also the formidable problem that all the parts may not evolve simultaneously. There is no way to show that they are formed in a single organism at the same time, such as the eye with its multiple parts. Finally, evolution is confronted with the quests of the origin and end of the process. Thus, there is no way to escape the question: the evolution of things may not have always been the same and that sometime in the future, design in nature may be demonstrated.

Also, it does not seem that Darwin contemplated what the political and social implications of his doctrine would be. His confidence in evolution must have been bolstered in by his alliance with Marx. The New Atheists, of course, are evolutionists and Marxists (of some variety inclined to the latter). Thus, taking his cue from Darwin, the biologist, Richard Dawkins, reduced humans to genes and atoms. He demolished the notion that humans were an inimitable species; and another Darwinist, Peter Singer, implored society to rid itself of the Christian moral code. The New Atheists would not disagree with him and, surely, would have strongly concurred that the abolition of the code would allow them to draw out the social implications of Marxian egalitarianism, that is, demolishes any notion of life's sanctity that is based on man's replication of the divine image and likeness. It is not difficult to understand that this abolition leaves open the permissibility of abortion and euthanasia. Evolution accommodates these medical practices if, in fact, it is not ultimately responsible for them, especially when "survival" seems to have become the only absolute value.

Furthermore, evolutionists are not prone to broadcasting their relation to eugenics (i.e., improving the human species by discouraging reproduction via persons with genetic defects and therefore eliminating the possibility of bearing or inheriting undesirable flaws). Atheists have found this science very useful. There are many, but we mention here only Mao Zedong. Like Marx, the Chinese dictator also denied the existence of a transcendent will. Also, he held that matter was the ultimate reality, meaning among other things, morality was an entirely human problem. He said that the systems of Darwin and Marx could be reduced to a single axiom: "rebellion is justified." At another time, Mao confirmed his Darwinism with the words "All demons shall be eliminated." His slaughter of seventy-eight million of his own people (including China's intellectuals and religious leaders) far exceeded the twenty million butchered by Stalin and Hitler's Auschwitz, Treblinka, Buchenwald, Sobibor, etc., and the six million European Jews. In his books, *China and Charles Darwin* (1983) and *Luxun and Evolution* (1998), James Pusey contends that the Englishman changed the Chinese politics forever and wrought a philosophical challenge against traditional Chinese beliefs. The story of Darwinism in modern China testifies to the roots of modern tyranny and the revolutions that bore them.

Prof. Jacques Barzun laments that "Newton banished God from nature, Darwin banned him from life, while Freud drove him from the last fastness, the soul."[21] He might have added the thought of Nietzsche, who offered a resolution to the ensuing nihilism for which he was largely responsible. He surely contributed to it with his scathing criticism of the contemporary culture, especially religion and morality. Not unlike Darwin, he presented a dynamic view of reality. Necessarily then, with the absence of a divine authority ("the death of God") to direct the behavior of humans, Nietzsche called for a rigorous "transvaluation of values." There was no other way to prevent the total breakdown of civilization that would, to be sure, unleash the forces of "pitiless barbarism." Now was the moment for the exceptional man—the artist, the philosopher, the scientist. The hope of humanity rests in the hands of the Übermensch, "the overman," the creator of values. He will be the model for others. He is not the "redeemer of men" but "the bearer of glad tidings."

Of course, Nietzsche repudiated "the Christ of faith" in favor of "the Jesus of history." He was the only Christian, and he died on the Cross, the philosopher once said. He was our Prometheus, who taught people to live fearlessly, robustly, and freely and subject to no tradition and no "slave morality." Nietzsche paid no attention to the Scriptures, to prophecy, because "God is dead." Although we are alone, we do not despair that man may find beatitude. For Nietzsche, natural selection was an invisible force, the "grace," as it was in the individual's quest. And to be sure, there were achievements of Greek antiquity to help us frame the future. If nothing else, it can teach those willing to aspire to a new plateau of culture the approval or disapproval of others is irrelevant. The Übermensch will need to be tolerated for his individual creativity and perfection as the only means to the general welfare in a world without God or the influence of religion. In *The Birth of Tragedy*, he declared that "the lone and cruel *uebermench*" is "the highest type of man," "the creative supremacist" who must triumph over the degenerate masses that retard his advance toward the achievement of human perfection.

"The goal of humanity," Nietzsche said, "cannot lie in its end, but only in its highest species."

It becomes clear now what the "death of God" signifies. Erasing God means not simply the utter secularization of the world but also coronation of a new ruler—man or, more precisely, the "highest species" of the human race. Consequently, the Church is inane and unwanted. As Bernard Ramm has put it, "the death of God" means "the emasculation and evisceration of the *Corpus Christiana*." We see already that Christianity is no longer the cultural norm and, as the historic foundation of Western culture, has vanished. There is more, if we may believe Martin Heideggar, "Nietzsche is announcing the end of the supra-sensory world, of which God is supposed to be its most real entity." We know that he is dead because as the Madman of *The Gay Science* asserts, "We have killed Him." His was a beneficial death because now, unshackled from the chains of God and Christianity, man is fully able to create his own destiny without the need of redemption nor a biblical or "slave morality." In our time, "the metaphysical God" has vanished.[22]

Freud eagerly read the German editions of Darwin's two internationally famous works, *The Origin of the Species* and *The Descent of Man*, and confessed that they had been the main reason for his deciding upon a career in science. He was convinced that Darwin had proved that the human race emerged from an unbroken line of the animal species, which gave to Freud, by virtue of that continuum, the idea that man did not have complete control over his mental processes. Furthermore, evolution, along with the "given structure of social groups," produced neurosis and, consequently, religion. Freud argued that "religion is comparable to neurosis which urges us to gain control of our environment." That effort leads to "the wish-world" out of which surfaced the notion of God. Much of recent antireligious polemic is inspired by Freud's early works. In his *God Is Not Great*, Christopher Hitchens cites Freud as an ally who supports his notion that religion is the property of weak-minded childishness. Psychologically, religious beliefs are the expression of "wish-fulfillment," desires that are the "fulfillments of the oldest, strongest, and most urgent wishes of mankind."

Darwin was not the only influence on Freud's thinking. Nietzsche was another figure of the nineteenth century who greatly impressed "the father of psychoanalysis" and Nietzsche by him. The three seemed to persuade one another. For example, the concepts of Nietzsche that intrigued Freud include the idea of the unconscious mind, of repression, and of dreams and illusions. Some of the latter's basic terms are identical to those of Nietzsche. We also notice a connection between Nietzsche and Darwin. As we know, the former held biological evolution to be the correct explanation for human history but also bearing on the far-reaching truths for both scientific cosmology and philosophical anthropology. He also agreed with Darwin that God is no longer necessary to account for the existence of the universe or the surfacing of our human species from prehistoric animals. Again, if we accept the explanations of traditional morality and the institutions with which they are associated, we must confront the implications for the status of extant social and religious values. Both argued that values are the constructions of our social world, deeply rooted in our unconscious, which means there are no objective moral values, nonindependent of the human mind and human societies. Albeit Darwin's influence on Nietzsche is evident, they did not entirely agree on the forces of evolution. They first saw them determined by the vigor of nature, the latter, taking this dynamic perspective to its logical conclusion, saw the relationship between the human species and its simian ancestors as temporary. It will be overcome by human creativity. Bergson agreed with him.

Finally, Freud, Darwin, Marx, and their successors, the New Atheists, are all the creatures of the same modernity with its own understanding of the individual, the self. They also have the same definition of the traditional spirituality and morality they have repudiated, indeed, which they have plundered. Necessarily then, reason has the same meaning for them, which involves man without a soul; and consequently, the idea of truth is really or more than the correspondence of subject and object. With this paradigm, truth has become virtually identified with science. If we believe that science has all the answers to all the great questions, there is no need for God, especially if we hold that religion is no more than a "social gospel" to feed and clothe the poor, to succor the widow, and to rescue the children.

There is something that this atheistic humanism has forgotten or, better, has never considered inasmuch as the West has long lost contact with the wisdom of the Church Fathers. Having revered them, having accepted their vision, there would have been no Scholasticism, no Cartesian revolution, no Kantian insurgency, no nineteenth-century historicism, and no contemporary materialism. The West with a patristic culture would have seen a different world. There would have been a different understanding of truth. As the Fathers declare truth is more than the offspring of the intellect *(dianoia)*; it is given by the divine Logos, "who enlightens every man that comes into the world." He is the source of truth, and truth is the mate of the soul. Even more, truth is therapeutic, the physician of the soul. So religious doctrine is much more than its formulation; it is necessary for the spiritual renewal of the individual, and Thomas Jefferson was wrong to think of it as "enslavement of the mind."

The nineteenth century is clearly the prolegomena to the New Atheism. However, the old atheists like their successors were not loud propagandists. Also, the latter had greater opposition, Christian scientists, German philosophers, and Romantic and British poets. Of course, some of these were atheists but rarely the poets and idealist philosophers. Samuel Taylor Coleridge and so many writers of this era were Platonists and, therefore, theists. They were also opponents to the developments in science (including evolution), which was commonly blamed on Hume.

There is also another matter: creativity that inhibits the progress of the physical sciences. The nineteenth-century utilitarianism, pragmatism, and positivism made no place "beauty," not with its materialism and mechanism. Henri Bergson hoped to overcome this impediment with his distinction between intelligence and instinct. He was not the only thinker who saw that materialist science would destroy creativity. We cannot forget the sophiology of the Russian philosophers, such Soloviev, Frank, Florensky, Berdiaev, etc., who saw in the secularization of history and thought "the decline of Western civilization."

THE NEW ATHEISTS

It does not seem that the New Atheists and their nineteenth-century antecedents were aware that both were vulnerable to the demands of philosophy's two basic doctrines: metaphysics (first principles) and epistemology (theory of knowledge). Materialist have no interest in defining and justifying the "first principles" of their science. Neither can they demonstrate how it is that they know what belongs to nature, especially when we consider that it can have no design or that there is nothing spiritual that has created and sustains it.

Why is it that Plato and the idealists are wrong? How can it be demonstrated philosophically that the universe is or is not wholly material, controlled by immutable natural laws, lacking the intrusion of things spiritual? Finally, if knowledge involves the object and subject, which has the primacy, and how are they related? Perhaps with Kant, we must say, "In the order of time, therefore, we have no knowledge antecedent to experience, and with experience all our knowledge begins" (*KdrV*, Int.,1). Knowledge is framed a priori by the mind, but it is awakened by "experience" or sense- data.

Kant is not the only thinker who believes that knowledge is noetic but that it is limited to human experience. Indeed, knowledge is purely rational and entirely rational. He is a philosopher, and that is the only way he can think about things. He knows nothing, as the others, of spiritual cognition (gnosis). He is right that knowledge is confined to being. He is also right that rational truth is necessary and universal (in space-time). Gnosis, of which scientists and philosophers know nothing, is "extra-experience"; and therefore, the question of God is beyond the scope of our "experience." It resides in the realm of the unknowable (noumenon). At the same time, we may reach him by faith. Faith is another level of "experience."

God is safe from the New Atheists. There is no way to encounter him, save through faith and piety. Inasmuch as they have neither, they have no access to the divine. Piety or what is often called ethics is not revealed; it is human and relative. They will not even consider right and wrong as an "antinomy." Free will is the basis of morality. The New Atheists have no place for freedom because the laws of nature make no room for it. In more than one debate, Christopher

Hitchens inquired whether it could not be showed that the atheist was as moral as the Christian. And of course, everyone conceded that could be. In truth, the atheist cannot be because he has no access to the first principle of morality: to love the Lord your God with all your heart and all your strength (Luke 10:27).

There is another way to look at this matter. In Dostoyevsky's novel *The Idiot*, his Prince Myshkin is an epileptic. He does not complain against God because of this affliction. His life's path might best be appraised according to the ideal—"Beauty will save the world." Beauty is much more than physical appearance, albeit the splendor of a sunset or the glorious peak of a mountain recalls this experience to be more than a physical encounter with transcendence; it identifies for the mind redemptive ways at that historical moment. It is something that fills the soul with something wonderful without words. We can feel it and see it and penetrate the mystery. We can, by our quest for truth and justice, incarnate beauty. Let it not be said that this may be achieved without grace. Through the novel, Dostoyevsky hopes to show that beauty of a person's inner self is aggrandized by its purgation from despair and pride. With Prince Myshkin, he shows that the sacred life is scarcely recognized by those around him, surely not those whose lives are violated by the passions. The ideals he holds within himself are the demonstration of the beauty that fills the soul. In this way, "Beauty will save the world" because the sacred soul fills it. Beauty takes on concrete meaning; and the leap of faith it summons no longer seems so remote, abstract, and sensuous. Finally, it comes to us that Christ is beauty.

CHAPTER I END NOTES:

[1] *God's Funeral.* New York, 1999, p. 11.
[2] *Ibid.*, p. 25.
[3] "Kierkegaard and Dostoevsky." In *Russian Philosophy III: Pre-Revolutionary Philosophy and Theology: Philosophers in Exile: Marists and Communists*, trans. J. M. Edie. Knoxville, Tennessee, 1984, p. 257.

4   Schweitzer, A. *The Quest of the Historical Jesus*, trans. F. C. Burkitt. Mineola, New York, 2010, p. 79.
5   Hegelians were divided into two camps, the Left and Right. The first was atheists (among whose number was Karl Marx) determined to eliminate traditional Christianity and the idea of transcendence. The second was the conservative Protestant proponents of Hegel's philosophy.
6   Strauss, D. F. *The Christ of Faith and the Jesus of History: A Critique of Schleiermacher's Life of Jesus*, trans. with introduction L. E. Keck, 1977, xxxii.
7   *The Essence of Christianity*, trans. G. Eliot with an introductory essay by Karl Barth and a foreword by H. R. Niehbuhr. New York, 1957, xxxvi.
8   *Ibid.*, p. 13.
9   *Ibid.*, xi.
10 *Ibid.*, pp. 50–51.
11 *Ibid*, p. 67. Augustine's *filioque* is a model for Feuerbach's trinity.
12 *Socialism: An Economic and Sociological Analysis*, trans. J. Kahane. Indianapolis, Indiana, 1981, pp. 289–295.
13 In his deliberations on materialism, Marx abolished the distinction between one man and another, even between human and nonhuman. It has the stench of Darwinism (see F. Kamenka, *The Ethical Foundations of Marxism*. London, 1972, p. 96f.).
14 "Contribution to the Critique of Hegel's Philosophy of the Right: Introduction." In *The Marx-Engels Reader*, intro. and trans. R. Tucker. New York, 1972, p. 12.
15 *Loc. Cit.* "On the Jewish Question," ibid., p. 29.
16 Engels, F. "Socialism: Utopian and Scientific," ibid., p. 606.
17 "The Age of Ideology: The Nineteenth Century Philosophers." New York, 1956, p. 161.
18 *Darwin, Marx and Wagner: A Complete Heritage*. New York, 1958, p. 52.

[19] "The Big Bang singularity does not represent a physical concept," asserts David Berlinsky, "because it cannot be accommodated by *physical* theory. It is a point at which physical theories give way." This concept in which so many have placed their confidence "is something that is either infinite and inscrutable, or otherwise unknown. Men have come to faith on the basis of far less." *The Devil's Delusion: Atheism and Its Pretensions*. New York, 2007, p. 81.

[20] *Darwin's God*. Grand Rapids, Michigan, 2002, p. 158.

[21] In Kevin Cole, *The Meaning of Nietzsche's Death of God*, 6 (Internet).

[22] Atheism cannot recognize the existence of the supernatural. It is by nature materialistic.

CHAPTER II

THE NEW ATHEISTS

Je n'ai pas besoin cette hypothese.
—Pierre-Simon Laplace

When Sam Harris published his remarkable *The End of Faith* in 2004, he gave voice to the new atheistic evangel. After two years, his *Open Letter to Christian America* was released. In quick order followed Daniel Dennett's *Breaking the Spell*, Richard Dawkin's *The God Delusion*, Christopher Hitchens's *God Is Not Great*, as well as Victor Stenger's *God: the Failed Hypothesis*. Of course, as religion was linked to "the God hypothesis," it necessarily became an object of scorn. Therefore, the New Atheists opposed animism, polytheism, henotheism, pantheism, as well as theism, especially Christian theism because it was the religion with which they were most familiar, the religion against that they primarily rebelled. Their nineteenth- century predecessors generally confined their atheism to the intellectual caste, but this new breed deliberately addresses its message to the mainstream reader. They bundled all religions together so that if one religion was wrong, all were the same. Their doctrinal differences are of no relevance. Daniel Dennett called upon academia to treat religion as merely another manifestation of some natural phenomena. Put another way, they turned their rage on whatever called for "faith" in the supernatural.

As the New Atheists contend, if there is obviously no personal God, there is palpably no revelation of him. In a word, religion is wholly subjective; and as church history shows, her teachings have brought nothing but pain and confusion and superstition to its adherents and the world. The origin of this harsh appraisal begins with the era of soi-disant "Enlightenment" in which the question of religious truth was seriously contested. That eighteenth- century movement swept away the medieval worldview and initiated the modern secular culture no better illustrated than the political revolutions of the last three centuries in which the king and the hierarchical social order were replaced by a new concept of the state with its humanist vision of history founded on "the ideals of liberty, equality and fraternity." It was Immanuel Kant's "What is Enlightenment?" that defined the movement as humankind's liberation from a self-inflicted immaturity, calling upon individuals to "think for themselves" (*sapere audi*). Accordingly, the Enlightenment tended to oppose any form of authority insofar as it competed with reason. Finally, it called for confidence in the process of self-directed thought and action, which must lead to a future of freedom and truth *sine termino* while at the same time throw free will into question. What else could be done if all reality is material? Indeed, what then happens to consciousness?

In his parable, *Nathan the Wise*, Gottfried Lessing (1729–1781) faced this problem relativistically. The poet compared God to a king who had three sons—Christianity, Judaism, and Islam—and who on his deathbed gave to each a ring (two of them fake) without telling them which ring was his. Lessing offered no solution, save that there is a true religion not really known to anyone. He may have suspected that hostility would rise between them but warned none of his sons. The proponents of the Enlightenment seemed not to take into consideration that Lessing's call for tolerance must lead to pluralism, bewilderment, war, and finally, general indifference to religion. Clearly, the idea of revelation would vanish and, of course, the idea of Jesus Christ as God incognito.

But if God is personal, if he revealed a religion to which he wanted all humanity to adhere, and if that religion was represented by one person, then obviously, he wears the "true ring," and the religion that he founded is the one and only true religion. It is a universal, maximal faith with absolute claims. And if it is the only divinely revealed religion, then it is the only religion with saving doctrine and practice. There is then some truth in the old adage, "All religions may be wrong, but only one can be right." If one religion is right, it is right by the will of God, and all others have been formed by human ingenuity and imagination. Again, if we argue that all religions are identical before him, we need to believe that truth is of no concern to him.

Then it may be argued too that if he is indifferent to religious truth, he has saddled humanity with contradictory faiths, a pronouncement that reveals something about his character not entirely worthy of a beneficent deity. A God of love and truth would necessarily deliver to his creatures a religion that reveals the divine and saving truth and beauty. Again, if there is no true religion, then Christianity has no more relevance to human life and thought than any other religion; and unavoidably, there is nothing unique in Christ, not his Crucifixion, Resurrection, ascension, or return for Judgment. Furthermore, the Christianity preached by the apostles is "illusory," to invoke Richard Dawkins. His disciples are deluded mystics. The teachings of the Fathers are wild conjecture dependent on the Greek speculation. Nevertheless, there is some evidence for Christian doctrinal veracity, such as its longevity, the perpetual experience of the martyrs, confessors, and the holy Fathers. The best evidence of all is the man himself.

Christ has brought not only the promise of salvation to the entire human race but also the "knowledge" of the one true God. He began the divine enterprise by a covenant with the Jews and then to the Gentiles. In the words of the Apostle Paul, "At that time you [Gentiles] were without Christ, being aliens from the commonwealth of Israel, and were strangers from the covenant of the promise, having no hope and without God (*atheoi*) in the cosmos" (Eph. 2:14). He subsequently established a new Gentile Israel. Here is what has been called the offense of particularity, "a scandal to the Jews and folly to the Greeks" (1 Cor. 1:23)[1] precisely because the claims of the Gospel are exclusive, thrown like a rock against the intellect.

If such an idea is not palatable, we have legitimate recourse to nothing but Dennett and others' characterization of Christianity as bigoted and supercilious, which gives credence to the calumny that the God of the Scriptures is nothing more than "moral monster" and that Christianity is indeed the most absurd lore. In their scheme of things, the New Atheists cannot allow that there is but one religion intended for the human race lest their treatment of religion appear a sham. In other words, if there is one true God and one true religion, then their proclamation that "religion poisons everything" falls to the ground. How could they argue that religion, especially the one maintaining a special relationship with the divine, is deleterious mirage? It is perhaps for this reason that the New Atheists carry an especially crude and spiteful hated for Christianity.

When Hitchens, Harris, Dawkins, etc., castigate religions, painting Christianity with the same brush as all other religions, they reveal more than the ignorance of the theology they condemn. In part, their cultural heritage is to blame, supplying them with the assumptions by which to build their case. Curiously, they referee all religions by personal (Western) standards of right and wrong, true and false, scarcely a position from which to build a prima facie case for their antireligious philosophy. They are hindered not only by their personal prejudices but also by a predetermined pastel paradigm of history and philosophy. Even more astounding is their application of a cultural inheritance with which they are not expert and oriental religions about which they are even less authoritative. In addition, "the Four Horsemen," etc., are not biblical scholars, or theologians, or historians, or linguists; and if they have any philosophical training, their biases bring no honor to the discipline. To mix serious argument with hate, sarcasm, and devious manipulation of the "evidence" is profitable to no one.

The New Atheists are not unaware that their doctrine requires an apologia. On this matter, we have Jason Scorse's "In Defense of Atheism and Free Thinkers," which appears in *Voices of Reason* (April

1, 2007); and Sam Harris brings "10 Myths—and 10 Truths—About Atheism" (*Los Angeles Times*, Dec. 24, 2006). Harris takes offense at the "myth" that atheists believe that life is pointless.[2] He maintains that eternal happiness beyond the grave is not the only way to give meaning to this life. To be sure, an atheist may impute importance to earthly life, but this is entirely personal, a choice with no predictable consequences. Yet Harris is content with his reverie of human life and finds "the fear of the meaninglessness ... well ... meaningless."

One may suspect that neither Scorse nor Harris have read Aldous Huxley (1894–1963) or heard his observation: "We don't know, because we do not want to know." Those who detect no meaning in the world generally do so because for one reason or another, it suits their purpose that the world should be "meaningless." As for Scorse, he agrees with Harris that life has "profound meaning." Evolution supplies it. On a more personal level, learning and experience expand one's consciousness. Whatever the basis of their beliefs, the atheist position is not secure. Evolution, as popular as it is among most scientists, is no more than a philosophical theory with a scientific facade. Even worse, they have provided no answers to the great epistemological questions that have haunted the Western intellectual tradition since Rene Descartes.

Harris challenges the "myth" that atheism has no genuine connection with science. One may suspect that his rebuttal is a "straw man." In truth, science has no necessary relation to atheism if only because historically, most Western scientists have been creationists (Newton, Maxwell, Carnap, etc.). And as is the nature of religious faith, it tends to erode when it is not prepared to meet the impressive achievement of scientific thinking. Again, an appeal to polls does not strengthen Harris's position: 90 percent of general U.S. public believes in a personal God, but 93 percent of the members of National Academy of Sciences do not. He does not show in his "10 Myths" that scientists who are atheists were not unbelievers before they undertook to study science. Moreover, science may be defined as the systematic examination of the structure and behavior of the physical world. To extend its province to include "the God hypothesis," as Dawkins wishes to do, is, in fact, to alter the conventional understanding of science and its metaphysical presuppositions. It does not further our discussion to insist that metaphysics has no relevance to science (or atheism) or because some savants think that it has long been discredited.

If we are to believe Sam Harris and his New Atheist cohorts, atheists are not arrogant. He apparently has not heard or read Richard Dawkins, who takes up any religious or ethical subject without contempt for it. Thus, it is with great nonchalance that Harris imagines that scientific probabilities provide a sound basis for the atheist's "happy, balanced, moral and intellectually fulfilled." Without justification, Professor Dawkins breaches the line between science and theology with a description of "the God hypothesis" as "a scientific hypothesis about the universe, which should be analyzed as any other proposition." His faith in science (reason) has persuaded him that all questions are ultimately scientific questions.[3]

It is surprising that his position is taken with so little "evidence." He speaks with such disdain about the haughtiness of religious people who are so secure in belief by virtue of their "election" to eternal life. We need not believe in predestination to observe that Dawkins has very little knowledge of theology and a short bibliography to prove it. Also, he aligns himself with Harris, who wants us to think that "when considering questions about the nature of the cosmos and our place within it, atheists tend to draw their opinions from science. This isn't arrogance; it is intellectual honesty." Inasmuch as science has no competence in spiritual matters, intellectual honesty would seem to demand that the scope of the empirical method would describe the range of science.

Myth 7 repels the notion that "Atheists are closed to spiritual experience." Harris received a PhD in cognitive neuroscience from the University of California. In his thesis, he insisted belief, disbelief, and uncertainty have a *neural basis*. He seems also to have received a BD in philosophy; but whatever he learned, it has not served him well, surely not in his denial of free will in man. He seems not to have considered that the rejection of freedom brings determinism with it. Necessarily then, whatever Harris believes has been predetermined. Perhaps he should have read Kant's transcendental dialectic and its antinomies on this matter. The Prussian's *Critiques* leave open the possibility that man's body, albeit constrained by the laws of nature, does not negate in man the noumenal or noetic power of creativity. Harris insists on dragging his evaluation of "sin" to support his concept of determinism. "Without free will, sinners would do just as poorly as calibrated clock work, and any notion of justice that emphasized their punishment …" New Atheists "do not need the illusions about a person's place in the causal order to hold him accountable for his actions or to take actions ourselves." A difficult position to hold if "free will is actually more than an illusion (or less) in that its paralysis cannot be verified scientifically, since no one has ever described a manner in which 'mental and physical events could arise that would attest to its existence.'"[4]

If Harris is right about neural foundations for belief, then unbelief, uncertainty, love and hate, and good and bad are chemical conditions of the human machine. By what means does he make any judgments about the freedom of the human will? If free will is no more than an "illusion," was it by chemical formula that he came to his conclusion about the want of free will? His entire network of anthropological categories is only assumptions drawn from the intellectual tradition of which he is a lifeless part. What does he know about the near and far East? Nothing he has written convinces the reader that he knows anything about the philosophy of Islam or Buddhism or Hindus or Confucianism. We must be puzzled that a materialist with so little knowledge of a world drenched in mysticism could say anything of significance about it. How does an evolutionist and positivist have any experience of a world so utterly opposed to his vision of the reality? Alan Watt's *The Way of Zen* (1985) might give him a clue. Perhaps worse, none of the New Atheists have shown any knowledge of that marvelous and forgotten Christian civilization—Byzantium—which Steven Runciman called "the greatest civilizing agency the world has ever known." Here was a time like no other in the history of the world where the inhabitants commonly took the deifying power of the Spirit for granted. Here was an eschatologically oriented realm, a culture steeped in mystery and intellect. The citizen lived in a kingdom dedicated to the propagation of the Christian faith, its emperor, the new Solomon, who with the ecclesial hierarchy together strove to perfect the people in that faith, which originated with the apostles.

It is intellectually dishonest for Harris et al. to criticize anything by which reason and its instrumentalities have no *droit d'entrée*. It is no wonder that with his mentality, there is no appreciation for anything that does not conform to his dark secular image. What else explains New Atheist's lack of tolerance for events that speak to us of a reality beyond scientific comprehension—the virgin birth of Christ or the Resurrection or the Eucharist? His ignorance notwithstanding, Harris insists, "These are just not the sort of claims that spiritual experience can authenticate." His "cognitive neural science" has a very narrow range of apprehension. He will not embrace such mysteries because he cannot. The lack of humility is the chief barrier to the world beyond the senses.

The eighth myth is "Theists believe that atheists hold that there is nothing beyond human life and human understanding." Harris replies, "Atheists are free to admit the limits of human understanding in a way that religious people are not." His remark is gibberish; he has not a centimeter of "understanding" of what they believe concerning their intellectual and spiritual inadequacy. He has presented no "evidence" that permits him to make absolute judgments about God, the cosmos, or man. Likewise, Harris's failures are clear: he lives by an unlimited faith in the future of the world prepared for the human race by the gargantuan authority of the physical sciences. Undoubted, this charge is irrelevant to him, and he continues to pile twaddle upon twaddle. He adds, "From the atheist point of view, the world's religions utterly trivialize the real beauty and immensity of the universe." This stand is a "stupidity before which even the gods are helpless."

Here is an amazing statement: "religions utterly trivialize the real beauty and immensity of the universe." What but religion has inspired the great music and art of the East and West? More than art and music, religion stands behind the development of science and medicine. Have Harris and his friends familiarized themselves with the relation among religion, economy, politics, and law? We have a right to wonder whether Harris and the other New Atheists have any comprehension of the world that stands behind Christian architecture, such as the Sistine Chapel, Hagia Sophia, Notre Dame in Paris, and St. Basil's of Moscow. Have they any knowledge of the effort made by monasticism in the spread civilization? Perhaps we are expecting too much from Harris, etc. And of course, he and his comrades have no familiarity with ancient Greek, Latin and Hebrew, Arabic, or Hindi languages. It makes no difference to them that Christianity, whatever its failures, whatever the evil it has perpetrated, has lifted the human mind (nous) to ethereal heights to which the atheist could scarcely imagine.

How can the New Atheist defend his ignorance? By diversion and by drawing on matters that give him an advantage in their disputes. In his ninth myth, Harris maintains that the "good effects" of all religions do not prove the truth of their doctrine and piety. His protest is not compelling. First, he cannot know what "good effects" are. His judgments about them are arbitrary. Only if there is one true and personal God may we speak of "good effects" with veracity, something only a spiritual man may judge. And if I have read philosophy correctly all these years, it would seem that reason demands that we define the idea of "good," a demand to which a Christian will never cede to ratiocination. Without the absolute "morality" (say, piety) of a divine standard of a personal and Almighty Being, there can be no "good." Mere human "good" (if there is such a thing) is relative and mutable; and the reward for atheism, as the modern world has manifested it, is nihilism.

Finally, Harris seeks to refute the tenth myth: "Atheism provides no basis for morality." Our reply has already been given. He repeats what he has said more than once, "We do not get our morality from religion." He will have a difficult time proving this contention, especially since the ethics of Western culture, his legacy, has been traditionally religious. Even Marxism has been unable to escape it. There is something hidden beneath Harris's proposition. Aldous Huxley has a valuable insight: "Atheists would not object to the Divine if it were not that in Western culture is identified with the Christian God,"[5] hence, "Christian morality." In addition, he portrays atheism as essentially "an instrument of liberation." One might wonder of what value is "liberation" to an automaton. Harris deflects the criticism with the comment, "We decide what is good in our good books by recourse to moral intuitions that (as some level) hard-wired in us and that have been refined through thousands of years of thinking about the causes and possibilities of human happiness." There is more to this uninformed speculation than meets the eye.

Of course, there is always the predictable excoriation of the wicked practices recounted in the "despicable" Bible and the Koran. He seems unconcerned, if not oblivious, to the fact that it is the departure of the "believer" from the moral code that accounts for his "wicked practices." It is not the influence of religion—surely, not Christianity—that brings on the deceit of the New Atheists. Dostoyevsky broadens the issue raised by this matter. In *The Brothers Karamazov*, he gives us a conversation among several men in a tavern:

> *And what do they talk about in that momentary halt in the tavern? Of the eternal questions, of the existence of God and of the immortality. And those who do not believe in God talk of Socialism or anarchism, of the transformation of all humanity on a new pattern, so that it all comes to the same end. They're the same questions turned inside out. And the masses, the masses of the most original Russian boys, do nothing but talk of the eternal questions! Isn't this so? ... You know, dear boy, there was an old sinner in the eighteenth century who declared that, if there were no God? He would have to be invented. S'il n'existait pas Dieu, il faudrait l'inventer. And man has actually invented God. And what is strange, what would be marvelous, is not that God should really exist; the marvel is that such an idea, could enter the head of such a savage, vicious beast as man.*

Not everyone would accept the existence of God for numerous reasons, such as the suffering of little children. There is no God, only man and the inventions of men. If that is the case, then we turn to atheism and atheism to socialism. "Atheists and socialists have more fantastic dreams than do believers. They aim at justice, but, denying Christ, they will end by flooding the earth with blood, for blood cries out for blood, and he that takes up the sword shall perish by the sword." Moreover, atheists are socialists because the latter is the only social order available to them. They have a compatible, if not the same, weltanschauung. They are blind who think of socialism as merely a labor program or atheism merely a theological point of view. To annihilate God is the first principle of their philosophy. To build the Tower of Babel is their goal, that is, not so much as to reach heaven but to bring it to Earth.

Returning to Dostoyevsky's *The Possessed*, he records the discourse by the atheist Kirillov. He says there is no God, and the world is under the control of its most resourceful and imaginative species: man. If he is in control and master of his fate, man is the earth's new god. As God and immortality do not exist, the new man is permitted to become god. If man is god, then he is the maker of values, the author of morality. Is there any way that his "divinity" may be affirmed? Life and death are in my hands. I can determine who lives and who dies, including me. Kirillov does not want God to exist, and he can prove it by the supreme act of will, his own suicide. "If God exists," he states, "all is His Will and from His will and I cannot escape. If not, it is all my will and I am bound to show my self-will."

> *Self-will? But why are you bound? Because all will has become mine. Can it be that no one on the whole planet, after making an end of God and believing in his own will, dares to express his own will on this most vital point? ... I am bound to show my unbelief, said*
>
> *Kirillov walking about the room. I have no higher idea than disbelief in God. I have all the history of mankind on my side. Man has done nothing but invent God so as to go on living, and not kill himself; that's the whole of universal history up until now. I am the first one in the whole history of mankind who would not invent God? Let them know it once and for all ...*

For three years, he has been looking for the attribute of his "godhead," and finally, he had found it. "The attribute of my godhead is self-will! That's all I can do to prove the highest degree of my independence and my new and terrible freedom. I am killing myself to prove my independence and my new terrible freedom." The irony is that this "the carnal god" must demonstrate his freedom and his will by his death. "The only result of this 'free action' is that he himself is the victim of his thoughts," writes Paul Roubiczek. "Overemphasis on the intellect has driven him to insanity."[7]

We may have no doubt that Dostoyevsky was aware of all the implications of atheism, including its "meta-ethical" or moral repercussions. He gives us three choices—Orthodox Christianity, socialism, or suicide. He relates in his famous parable of *The Grand Inquisitor* what the consequences of socialism are: the loss of freedom for the sake of "miracles, mystery and authority," that is, man needs to be astonished, awed, and protected. The state will give him these things. If there is no God and suicide is not an option, what is left but socialism? Socialism is not merely a question of the working class but also, above all, the quest for utopia. According to Dostoyevsky, socialism is a materialistic philosophy that cannot accomplish its purpose without destroying the moral world. He calls it madness to attempt the erection of a nation or a world or an empire on the principles of science or reason. In a word, socialism is quintessentially atheism. The New Atheists have chosen socialism over suicide.

Sam Harris and his coven of atheists live by abstractions. Morality is not the least of them. Nevertheless, they have every intention to live by them. Thus, Christopher Hitchens boasts that an atheist can be as moral as a Christian; and of course, he points to their hypocrisy to prove it. There are several replies to Hitchens's boast. First, if there is no absolute standard of right and wrong, there is no reason for such a comparison. Second, if there is a personal God, the atheist cannot be moral while denying the first principle of morality: "Love the Lord your God without all your heart, with all your strength and your entire mind" (Luke 10:27). Finally, if there is a God, the atheists have no divine grace and cannot achieve dispassion (apatheia) without which there is no access to him. But then if they recognize the action of the passions within them, they turn them into "creative forces" as Descartes exhorted. They have nothing but the hope that one day there will come the vindication of their ideology, the moment when all their scientific principles and propositions have been justified, especially their moral canons, whatever they may be.

As it has been said more than once, without God as the ground of morality, there can be none at all. In fact, his absence leaves us with the task of defining the word, and we may be assured not everyone will agree on the definitions. Furthermore, if there is no accepted system of morality, there is nothing morally valuable, including man himself. It follows there is no normative force, nothing to regulate social order and to bring on personal perfection. The New Atheists' belief that they have an answer for this dilemma is a shot in the dark. Dawkins relies on evolution and natural selection to develop moral values by which everyone will eventually live in contentment. He depends on the action of atoms and genes to explain the morality and happiness, more of Dawkins's "puerile mystification." He extends the powers of natural selection beyond its specified purpose. In truth, "It only eliminates, or tends to eliminate whatever is not competitive," writes Anthony Flew. "Consequently, the variation within or between species promises no competitive advantage relative to extinction."

Of course, not everyone will accept "Darwinian reasons" for human altruism, in particular, via the calculus of natural selection. For Dawkins, the evolutionary process is the progenitor of morality. It manipulates the brain with its chemistry to induce ethical behavior. Apparently, it is not very successful inasmuch as there is no evidence that it does. He has forgotten that "altruism" is not the ordinary way for most humans. They must assume that evil is a chemical imbalance. My suspicion is that he has little or no understanding of "virtue" or of immorality, a fortiori of religious piety. He protests against the religious "policing" of individual behavior. Dawkins delivers no homily on things corrupt, the shameless, and the merciless, that is, the sinner. It seems unlikely that he would agree with St. Irenaeus of Lyon that government was instituted among men "to restrain evil."

Sam Harris postulates that whatever contributes to "well-being" or "peace and tranquility" is morality (eudemonism). There are too many things of which he and his colleagues do not take into account. There never has been and never shall be such a circumstance in which men by their limited knowledge can realize the happiness we all want. Again, humanly conceived morality will always change. It is futile to argue that a moral consensus has never been found in religions. But that is the point. There can be no universal morality without a universal religion and no universal religion without one true and universal God. To envisage the future beatitude of human nature as Harris, etc., do, it will never come to pass because the obstacle to its realization is degenerate man. Undoubtedly, it is a notion for which he has nothing but disdain. Morality—no, piety—is intended to alter human nature, but there is no human instrumentality by which this may be accomplished. As St. Symeon the theologian insists, virtue (piety) is the transformation of our nature from the mortal to the immortal, the corrupt to the incorrupt (*Disc.* XXXIII, 78–86). The New Atheist persistently argues that God does not exist; therefore, supernatural intervention is a delusion of the superstitious mind, none worse than the mind of the Christian.

True morality is ascetical; it begins with self-denial. It is neither Ayn Rand's hyper-individualism nor George Lukacs's collectivism. In the first place, morality is not the word the Church Fathers employ but piety (*eusebia*), which includes not only "dispassion" (purging of the passions) but also adherence to revealed doctrine. It is the life of repentance or the wrestling against the evil one, that is, "separation from this world" (2 Cor. 6:14–15). Piety is possible only in the Church if the Church is indeed a divine race. The purpose of piety is to achieve communion with God, that is, to become "partakers of the Spirit," to cite St. Symeon the New Theologian says (*Disc.* XV, 6). With him comes dispassion and preparation for participation in the divine nature (2 Pet. 1:4)—*theosis.*

My intention in discussing the Scriptures is not to parry each thrust of the New Atheists. Their numerous books, among other things, are intended to demolish the basis of scriptural theology and piety, that is, the supernatural. Their motive has never been to find the truth in the manner of the scholar but play the role of an iconoclast. Their attack upon a traditional source Christian theology is to demonstrate the veracity of atheism. We recognize that their pettifogging of the Bible is, among other things, to strike down the idea that religion is the origin of morality and, consequently, to propagate disbelief in its God, which begins with abrogation of the deity they fear and despise.

For Richard Dawkins, the Bible is "the same weird volume that religious zealots hold up as the inerrant source of our morals and rules for living."[8] His bibliography on this subject is unimpressive. He calls upon the infamous Anglican "Bishop" John Shelby Spong "master of confusion and misinterpretation" as a witness to his cause. Dawkins and the other New Atheist examine the Bible not for wisdom but for incidences and rhetoric that corroborate their prejudices. The New Atheists did not take the time to study the diverse methods of biblical exegesis, certainly not the treatment of the Scriptures by the Fathers of the Church.[8] There is the literal method ("following the letter") and least common means of biblical exegesis; also, the typology or comparisons between Old and New Testaments persons and events (e.g., Moses prefigures or typifies Christ, ancient Israel adumbrates the Church, the blood of the lamb the Eucharist, the Red Sea baptism); and finally, allegory or persons, places, and rites understood as symbolic truths (e.g., Abraham as a symbol of faith). These three methods are not always employed.

The New Atheists do not handle the Old Testament texts with care, failing to place "stories of interest" within the context of a powerful moral vision. They look at God as a "cosmic Dictator" and the Ten Commandments as a "moral tyranny." They have no sympathy with Hebrew piety and its development. The New Atheists give no consideration to the witness of the Old Testament as "the preparation for the Gospel" as the story of Israel leading to something ontologically greater to an ethic that anticipates a religion of love (Jer. 31; Ezk. 36). Moreover, they pay no attention to the fact that the authors of the numerous books have a personal style, often tendentious, inclined to exaggerate victories and losses, decorating the truth with hyperbole.

Aware of their special place in the divine economy, the Israelites shaped their language to punctuate that privilege and divine favor.

Nevertheless, the significance of their narrative does not conflict with the revelation given them by God. Their conviction is palpably not shared by the New Atheists. What is interesting is the remark of Sam Harris, who delights in throttling Old Testament theology and devoutness. He makes the unfortunate remark that "the practitioners of the various barbarisms that persist around the globe cannot be judged by the standards of the West, nor can people of the past be judged by the standards of the present."[9] This does not strengthen the New Atheists case against the Old Testament.

The New Atheists are constitutionally unable to grasp the simple and fundamental fact that God is beyond rational knowledge. For reasons we do not know, he created man and the world, and he rules them. He is not to be judged; he is the adjudicator. Whatever he does is good and true even if we cannot always comprehend it. Let us remember the words of Gerhard Tersteegen, "A comprehended God is no God" or, better, the words of the prophet, "'For my thoughts are not your thoughts, neither are your ways my ways,' the Almighty reveals to Isaiah. 'As the heavens are higher than the earth, so are my ways higher than your ways'" (Isa. 55, 8–9 LXX). His transcendence implies his sovereignty as well as his incomprehensibility. Moreover, his prerogatives as Creator place his actions beyond human verdicts.

It is not difficult, therefore, to imagine that Sam Harris would bark, "The God of Abraham is a ridiculous fellow—capricious, petulant, and cruel—and with whom a covenant is little guarantee of health or happiness."[10] What else could account for epithet "God is a monster"? There are numerous biblical episodes that repel our New Atheists. Their inept responses satisfy them, and they accept no reasonable objection to their biblical meddling; hence, all the debates at Oxford or Boston or Edinburgh have become showcases for their daring eloquence. No wonder the Tower of Babel is a fable, the story of Moses and Israel a myth, and everything else an indictment of patriarchal sexism.[11] How else to explain Yahweh's "morbid obsession with sexual restrictions"?[12] The New Atheists have not the slightest understanding of chastity or virginity and their relevance to communion with God.

THE NEW ATHEISTS

A little more attention must be given to the New Testament Christ. The New Atheists, of course, deny his divinity. One might expect that they would have consulted Albert Schweitzer and his school as a valuable resource, but they are not indexed in their books. While raising the old notion that he may never have existed, Dawkins generously concedes that "the historical evidence for Jesus existence is slight." What is said to be known about him is described as "alleged facts." He simply discounts the details of his life recorded in the Gospels and the letters to Saints Paul, John, James, and Jude. [13] Maybe it is pointless to cite the words of the Lord, "The Father and I are one" (Jn. 10:30) or "Before Abraham, I am" (Jn. 8:58); St. Thomas's exclamation, "My Lord and my God" (Jn. 20:28); and his words to St. Paul on the road to Damascus, "Saul, Saul, I am Jesus Who you are persecuting" (Acts 9:5). The words "I am" identify the God with whom Moses spoke on Mt. Sinai (Ex. 3:14).

The historical record of Christ's divinity is not the only aspect of the Scriptures to suffer under the "deconstruction" of the New Atheists. Naturally, they deny the virgin birth of the Savior that, incidentally, had been opposed early in history of Church and is repelled by St. Jerome in *Contra Helvidius* and *Contra Jouvianus*. Not having read this Father's defense of Christ's unique birth, the New Atheists endorse the opinions of some modern scholars that the Greek rendering of Isaiah 7:14 ("Behold a virgin …") is false. The Hebrew word *Alma* (young woman) has been wrongly translated into the Greek by *parthenos* or the English word for "virgin." According to Sam Harris, the rendering of "virgin" is the result of the Church's "anxiety about sex." In fact, she must be a virgin if Christ is the "second Adam," who is the new beginning. Her virginity blocks Christ's inheritance of the "first Adam's" mortality.

Further "evidence" against the virgin birth is ostensibly the absence of the episode in the Gospels of Mark and John.[14] Failing to research the difference between the Gospels, he came to this premature conclusion. Each of them points to a dimension of the Lord's nature and purpose, his significance for Israel and the world. For instance, Mark shows that Jesus was "the Servant," hence, the

Messiah. John proclaims him as God as "the Word (Logos) was made flesh and dwelt among us."

This is clearly implied in the words of St. Paul (Gal. 4:4): "But when the fullness of time was come, God sent His Son, made of a woman, under the Law." The next assault comes against the redemption of Christ. Assuming the persistent "theology of the Cross" in the West during the last millennium, the New Atheists predictably refer to his sacrifice as "the atonement"—Christ "atones" for humanity's sin through his Crucifixion.[15] The basis of their critique of Christology, if nothing else, is part of the New Atheists cultural legacy. There is here the postulation, inasmuch as theology and Christology are linked, that the elimination of the one is the elimination of the other. In this, we may concur with them.

The New Atheist ridicule of the Scriptures betrays a defiance of the evidence given in the archeological record, for example, the historicity of Sodom and Gomorrah, which not so long ago was confirmed.[16] It is they who are the hypocrites for refusing to follow the "evidence" where it leads. It is no exaggeration that they are indifferent to anything that is not congruent with their aims, that is, to discredit the Old and New Testaments that they believe will also "tear the legs out" from under Christian theism. The New Atheists have not been alone in this ambition. Their predecessors had the same aspiration and provided the same arguments against the history and doctrine of the sacred books and, therefore, discredit theism.

The New Atheists have other objections, especially the place of Christ who have argued that there is no proof that he ever existed. Of course, there is no evidence that he was crucified and rose from the dead. Christopher Hitchens inquired that if he was the Savior of the world, why did he take so long to come? Many people suffered and died who might have been saved if he had been with us from the beginning. Hitchens might not have asked this query if he had a little more understanding of the divine economy or plan. As we have said, he was always with the human race, guiding it, inspiring it, and enlightening it, especially among his Chosen People, which prepared the world for his Incarnation, the final step in God's redemption. Even the pagans contributed to his coming.

There is too much we do not know about God and his plan to rescue humanity from death and its sins. Surely, his wisdom is beyond human understanding. There is no analogy between human and divine ways. If eventually, God and man are alike, immortal and incorrupt, it is because man is deified by grace or the uncreated energies (2 Pet. 1:4). The New Atheists have no knowledge of this soteriology. Deification was once part of Western culture. Now with its secularization, if that is to be accomplished, it would seem that the transformation of man belongs to the dynamic of biological evolution. We cannot forget that Nietzsche was indebted to Darwin for much of his thinking about the development of man. There is no reason to doubt that if man progresses, he might very well become what Nietzsche called Übermensch. Such a notion is perfectly consistent with the philosophy of the New Atheists.

To Nietzsche, they are grateful for unshackling man from "the chains of God and Christianity," and humans are now fully able to create their own destiny without the need of redemption these offer. Their "slave morality" is likewise abolished. Where we go after "the death of God" is the individual's achievement. Thus, the phrase "the death of God" means for the New Atheists all the reasons for their rejection of Christianity. It also means the heralding of a new epoch, the end of end of the Christian era in which, Hitchens held, that religion is at best irrelevant and at worst irrational, that is, poisonous.

More than one scholar wonder why the New Atheists praise the work of Nietzsche when they owe him so much. In part, they do not want to be linked with a philosopher who was associated with Nazism. One thing is certain, Nietzsche was neither a liberal nor a Communist. Yet both have the same principles, especially in their opposition to Christianity. Both seek a new worldview. There probably would not have had a modern atheist without Nietzsche, and it would not have spread without the New Atheists. And indeed, both announce the end of the spiritual world of which God ostensibly is the most real entity. Finally, they both seek a "revaluation of values." Both must insist that if God no longer lives, traditional morality is dead as well.

Atheists hope to avoid nihilism, but that would seem impossible in an egalitarian society. Socialism seems always to produce tyranny. Perhaps that is a reason that the New Atheists favor "cultural Marxism." To that end, they turn for help from physiology, psychology, and chemistry. Such inquiry may show some way to control human behavior. Moral absolutes are the only hope for peace and contentment, but they cannot provide them. The New Atheists cannot promise any, not in the form of Communist China and Russian or in Castro's socialism.

CHAPTER II END NOTES:

1. There is more to this matter, but it has been reserved for the last chapter.
2. He must not have read the statistics that atheists commit suicide in greater number than people affiliated with religious communities. See Dervic, K., etc., "Religious Affiliation and Suicide Attempt," *American Journal of Psychiatry*, CLXI (2004): 12, 2303–2308.
3. *The God Delusion*, pp. 23–24.
4. *The End of Faith*, pp. 272–273.
5. *Ends and Means*. London, 1946, p. 273.
6. *The Misinterpretation of Man: Studies in European Thought in the Nineteenth Century.* London, 1947, p. 235.
7. *The God Delusion*, pp. 268–269.
8. Dawkins mentions St. Gregory Thaumatourgos ("miracle worker") only to criticize him, saying whatever miracles may have won him his nickname, they were not miracles of honest lucidity. "His words convey the characteristically obscurantist flavor of theology." Since the eighteenth century theology has refused to develop ... unintelligible propositions. It is the mere Abracadabra of the mountebanks calling themselves the priest of Jesus" (*The God Delusion*, pp. 54–55). As the rest of the New Atheists, Dawkins knows nothing about the theology or the history of it. In fact, he does not know its origin or purpose. His ignorance of the

Fathers is blatant. He does not know what a saint is, and it is not his desire to learn. It would have been better if he dealt with things within his competence, such as biology.
9. *The End of Faith*, p. 179.
10. *Ibid.*, p. 173.
11. *The God Delusion*, p. 56. God is neither male nor female, and if the Lord is called he, it is because this pronoun is used in the Scriptures; hence, "he" chose it.
12. *Ibid.*, p. 58.
13. *The God Delusion*, pp. 117–118. Cf. Christopher Hitchens, *God Is Not Great.* New York, 2007, ch. 8; *The End of Faith*, pp. 22–24, 94; D. C. Dennett, *Breaking the Spell.* New York, 2006, p. 51f; V. J. Stenger, *The New Atheism: Take a Stand for Science and Reason.* Amherst, New York, 2009, pp. 58–66.
14. *The End of Faith*, pp. 95–94.
15. *The God Delusion*, pp. 286–287.
16. Price, R., *The Stones Cry Out: What Archaeology Reveals About the Truth of the Bible.* Eugene, Oregon, 1997, pp. 109–124.

CHAPTER III

THE NEW ATHEISTS AND THE TRUE GOD

O the depths of the riches both of the wisdom And knowledge of God! How unsearchable Are His judgments and His ways past Finding out?
—Romans 11:33

Debate and discussions about God generally fail to identify him; or if they do, they mistakenly identify him with the abstract "God" of theism, the so- called Supreme Being. It is with a certain humor that they call upon Christians, Muslims, and Jews, who, as they say, are already "atheists" by their rejection of the Greek gods and Asian polytheism, to perfect their position by repudiating the Christian God. Interesting, if not ironical, is that atheists have not understood that their atheism has converted human beings to the supreme beings on Earth. It is reason, the power that only man possesses elevates him to the station of divinity. In addition, they are unaware that the true believer differentiates between the Christian theology or triadology (Holy Trinity) and the theology of all other religions. The New Atheists have no understanding of Christian exclusivism, that is to say, as declared in the Lord's declaration, "This is eternal life that

THE NEW ATHEISTS

you may know the only true God and Jesus Christ whom He has sent" (Jn. 17:3).

Put another way, the difference between an atheist and a Christian is not the force of logic but a vision of reality that for atheism is materialism, naturalism, and monism, nothing supernatural, nothing transcendent, while for the Christian, reality is the unity of matter and spirit, the paradoxical unity of the human and the divine: the Incarnation of Christ Jesus as the embodiment of that unity. The former is created, while some things spiritual are uncreated. In a word, reason is not the arbiter of truth, and the physical sciences ("natural philosophy") are not the ultimate source of *knowledge*. Whatever the New Atheists may propose, they are materialists, and their entire vision depends on reason's reaction to the senses. Thus, they recognize nothing ideal or spiritual and, therefore, no God.

At the same time, we cannot explain the usual debates over the "existence of God" that ignores the identity of God as the Holy Trinity. I have yet to hear an argument that justifies atheism in terms of anti-Trinitarianism. How strange too that the Christian debater ordinarily often fails to place the Trinity at the center of his apology. The theists may fear perhaps that the idea of God as Trinity brings a religious bias into the debate. I have read that the New Atheists hold with Nietzsche that "God is dead," and the Trinity is impossible. I do not recall hearing from the atheists a philosophical refutation of the Christian worldview at the heart of which must stand Father/Son/Holy Spirit. Such a task demands a greater knowledge of Christian theology than they usually provide.

Occasionally, casually, the New Atheists confess the relevance of a worldview to their arguments; but I have yet to hear them openly exposit their position of their first principles. The New Atheists or Four Horsemen (Sam Harris, Christopher Hitchens, Richard Dawkins, and Daniel Dennet, etc.) show their antagonism toward the "supernatural," but they offer no *evidence*, an interesting word, of its nonexistence. And of course, they concede that nothing is transcendent, while consciousness and all things relative to it are reduced to proteins and the dance of atoms. Some ancient Greek philosophers took the same position and also failed to persuade their contemporaries.

David Bentley Hart refers to these modern "theologians" as "suave and fatuous." In their debates with "the Four Horsemen," Christians fail to vigorously challenge their "first principles" and back the spirituality of their own religion. They ought to have set to the front of their challenge to the New Atheist the doctrine of the Christian truth and its implications for creation and redemption. It is not enough to quarrel that Christianity bases her claims from "the evidence," such as the historical Resurrection of Christ. Christians ought to defend their faith not on the foundation of different interpretations of the same "evidence" (which the New Atheists are permitted to define) but to reiterate the difference between their worldviews. It should be obvious that the dispute rests on *phenomena bene fundata*. Using words of Albert Camus, they ought to be charged with propagating "truth not phenomena."

The silence of the New Atheists on the nature of knowledge is significant. It is clear that reason (ratio, *dianoia*) alone cannot promise satisfying answers to anything without first demonstrating what knowledge is (epistemology) and, of course, recognizing that it is not reason that always accounts for the truth of the matter. One never hears that the New Atheists provide us with a "critique of pure reason." In large part, they are influenced by the notion that only science provides the truth. And of course, where they offer any discussion of knowledge, it is devoid of the spiritual element because all knowledge is presumed to acquire by the action of the senses. One need not wonder if they have any acquaintance with "knowledge more than human," a *"gnosis"* as St. Paul and the Fathers call it. Transcendent truth comes to the human mind by *"gnosis"* and "gnosis" by divine enlightenment. Enlightenment is initiated at baptism. Grace and enlightenment are augmented by "dispassion" *(apatheia)*.

Let me repeat what I have said before about theology but with insights of my old friend, the French Orthodox theologian, Father Patric Ranson. To be sure, theology demands a quest for the true God and also the extirpation of the passions. Moses is the model of the theologian. He removed his shoes before approaching the burning bush, that is, contemplation (*theoria*) requires purging of the passions, in other words, before admitted into the presence of God or what St. Gregory of Nyssa describes as the "luminous darkness" by which God often reveals himself. The relationship between God and the theologian demands quest and love. Intellect provides the verbalization of the religious experience. The Fathers have nothing in common with Augustine, Aquinas, Calvin, or Karl Barth.

We need to distinguish between "the one true God" and the philosophical god, which commonly, the New Atheists mistakenly equate with theism. I suppose it makes little difference to them what they malign and despise, just so long as it is not supernatural or mystical. If nothing else, their lack of discrimination demonstrates the poverty of their scholarship. In this regard, their indifference to patristic theology is greater evidence of their superlative pretensions in matters over which they smugly claim to have mastery. Furthermore, they have assumed that their conception of knowledge and apprehension of truth have been undertaken with a "pure reason." Moreover, they have shown no understanding of the relation between language and reality. Finally, they have no idea that if God exists, he is a mystery and therefore beyond the ability of human reason either "to say or to show" (Wittgenstein). In other words, they fail to recognize that their metaphysical presuppositions determine their understanding of time, space, and existence.

There is something in the debate over the existence of God that is always ignored probably because the antagonists have never thought of it: the paradox of triadology. Surely, it has never entered the minds of the New Atheists that God is much more than a supernatural being. In fact, he does not fall within the category of being as Augustine, Anselm, Aquinas, etc., insisted. As the Fathers insist, God is "beyond being" (*hyperousios*). If he did, we would need to admit it is certain comparability between the God and the things he has created—*analogia entis*. For example, Augustine compared the Holy Trinity (Father, Son, and Holy Spirit) to the human mind (memory, intellect, will). It is from this theological paradigm the *filioque* (i.e., the Holy Spirit proceeds from the Father *and the Son*) emerges.

Moreover, if the supreme being of God and the created being of man are analogous, as Western theology has traditionally claimed, he may be judged (to some degree) by the very morality his creatures are judged. It is by this analogy that the New Atheists justify their criticism of God as "moral monster." To him is presumptuously applied a code of morality that he demands as Creator for those who follow him. Whatever they presume to say about God, it is arbitrary and inadequate. In any case, they are not spiritually prepared to say anything about him or the religion he has revealed. They seem not to know that the Trinity lives at a radically different level of reality. He is beyond judgment.

What might they learn if they examined the mysticism of the Church Fathers. In his *De Incomprehensibili*, St. John Chrysostom declares, "We call Him the inexpressible, the unthinkable, the invisible, the inapprehensible: who quells the power of human speech and transcends the grasp of all mortal thought; and also inaccessible to the angels, unbeheld by the Seraphim, unimagined by the Cherubim, invisible to principalities and authorities and powers; and, in a word to all creation" (PG. 48 721). Chrysostom represents the theology of all the Fathers, that is, apophatic (negative) doctrine of God, which St. John of Damascus maintains has been traditioned from the apostles (*De Fid. Orth.* I, 1 PG. 94 789B). They distinguish theology from "the economy" or the revealed doctrine and mystagogy of the Church.

At the same time, the God whom the Church worships is in himself unknowable, not merely unknown. He has no name, not even "being," which is often employed by the Fathers for want of name. Also, too many people are ignorant of the fact that the Father alone is called God, while the Son and the Spirit emerge from him, the Son begotten of him, the Spirit "spirating" from him. Again, the Fathers do not presume, as so many medieval and modern thinkers, to analyze the divine nature in terms of his attributes. It is his uncreated energies, not his incomprehensible essence, that bear his attributes and names. The energies or operations emerge from each person and thereby imply that God is "incomprehensible" even to the angels. How is the unknowable knowable? "For the knowledge (*gnosis*) of God's existence has been implanted by Him in the creature by nature," writes St. John of Damascus (l.c.). We also know that he exists by revelation. The seed of knowledge is sewn in each individual by the Logos, the second person of the Holy Trinity, who became man. Also, God is reflected in every aspect of physical nature, a truth first stated by the Apostle Paul. In addition, atheism (denial of his "existence") and idolatry (false conception of God) are viewed by the Apostle as the result of sin (Rom. 1:20).

The New Atheist has failed to understand that "in the beginning," even if his creative activity began with the "big bang," was, in fact, God the Son, the preincarnate Logos and, furthermore, that he was always among men; indeed, the Logos who formed all things eventually fulfilled his plan for them by his Incarnation, the Cross, and Resurrection. Before "the fullness of time," he was among men as the light of truth. He enlightened every man who came into the world (Jn. 1:9), especially, such as Noah, Job, Plato and Aristotle, Amenhotep, Laozi, Buddha, etc. His plan for man's redemption began with the Jews. The Redeemer, the Messiah came from the Jews not only as prefigures or types, such as Adam and Eve and Christ or "the Second Adam" and the Church, the Ark as the prefigurement of the church, the Passover or the Eucharist, etc. His birth was the realization of the divine plan for the recovery of the universe and the grand evidence that there is one God, a personal God whose purpose for the creation was its recovery from the forces of evil that had assaulted the things of time and space from the moment of the first man's disobedience.

The fallen angel, the devil, became the "god of the age," incessantly intruding upon the relationship between the Creator and the creature. If we may cite St. Paul, the Incarnation is "the mystery of His Will, that in the fullness of times He might gather together in one all things in Christ" (Eph. 1:10), that is to say, to recover the cosmos from the demons and thereby to reunite the personal Creator and the creature. In the words of the Apostle Peter, the Divine-human relationship describes man's "participation in the divine Nature" (2

Pet. 1:4) or, in the parlance of the Church Fathers, "deification" or "divinization" (*theosis*). So it is that the existence and character of God are revealed in history through the mystery of His *Oikonomia* (plan of salvation).

Here was the original Christian message (Gospel) that has been corrupted by secular philosophy, largely through Greek ideas. The first tenet of Christian wisdom, its theology, was corrupted by those who hoped to emasculate the Gospel and adapt it to secular philosophy. Often, those calling themselves Christian ignore the words of the Scripture, which declares, "The faith is once delivered to the saints" (Jude 5). Nevertheless, the question will be asked (as it must) whether this or any other God exists. Strangely, it is only in the West where the existence of the divine is an intellectual problem, which is precisely what the New Atheists have made of it. How is that they think, even as their debates and books show, that his existence is imaginary, illusory, that their arguments are therefore sufficient to eviscerate the illusions of theism, in particular, the Christian God about which they know very little?

The rational and systematic reconstruction of the divine and things divine necessarily alter the Christian message and the nature of the Christian religion itself. Of course, secularism is the contemporary transformer, but it is difficult to believe that emasculation of Orthodox Christianity did not begin with Descartes. Defining God as the "Supreme Being" and Christ in non-Chalcedonian terms opened the way to the mysticism of Meister Eckhart and Jacob Boehme, Spinoza and Schelling, Leibnitz and Newton, Hegel and Kant, etc. The point of departure in post-patristic theology is, as Heidegger contends, the concept of being (*ens*). The Fathers referred to God as beyond being (*hyperousios*), that is, beyond knowledge inasmuch as being is the object of knowledge. For the Scholastics and those who followed, whatever their configuration of God, it begins with the notion of being. Always the purpose is the construction of a new world and a new man. Eventually, that end came to center on "the historical Jesus" if we may believe Albert Schweitzer *cum sui* who made "the quest of the historical Jesus." It was the nineteenth century when the "historical" and "divine Jesus" became a serious dispute. This distinction was justified on the basis of the metaphysic of becoming. Support came from Darwinian evolution with the notion of incessant change. On the other hand, if Christ is the Incarnate Lord, history has another meaning, *coincidentia oppositorum*, the permanence and change of and unity of things spiritual and material dimensions.

Who then is this "Supreme Being" who permeates all things by his uncreated energies? Is he transcendent in nature, the incomprehensible, the infinite who dwells in the mystery of an inapprehensible glory beyond the duality of spirit and matter? He is hidden from the phenomenal realm, that is to say, he is not comprehended within the province of the senses. He is impervious to the demands of the sciences that all "evidence" must be empirical and positivist. In other words, the knowledge of him requires a suprarational type of evidence. He reveals himself to the seeker and pious. Anything else must obviate patristic metaphysics.

Historically, the pretensions of reason have generated a positive or *kataphatic* theology (God is …). It has transposed what had been the fruit of contemplation into the "problem" of God, that is to say, into a "problem" for the philosophical intelligence, metaphysical and linguistic, and therefore a departure from traditional or patristic theology. Instead of fidelity to the apophatic or negative method (God is not …) of those upon whose shoulders Western thinkers once claimed to sit, the Scholastics and their successors equated God with "being" from whom are deduced all his attributes (*virtutes*), which define his "active essence," that is, consistent with his absolute unity and simplicity. God as being has fallen within the domain of logic from which came not only "proofs" for his existence but also the presumptuous analysis of his nature with which his persons are identified.

From the idea that God qua being was born the *filioque*, that is, the Holy Trinity as the Spirit of God emerging from the Father *and the Son* acting as one principle, and this ultimately from the idea that the human mind is icon of God. It was Augustine who equated the three persons with the divine essence. The Father, Son, and Holy Spirit became three "opposed relations," two of which, the Father and the Son, united as one principle to exude the Holy Spirit.

As Thomas Aquinas affirmed, "In God relations and essence do not differ from one another, but are the same" (*Sum. Theol.* I q. 28 a. 2). It follows that the essence of God is an "active essence." This had no place in the apostolic tradition that, as already has been said, was the *apophatic* theology of the Church Fathers.

To encounter him, it is not a matter of logic but of the spiritual condition of the "theologian." To "know" anything about God requires a regenerate "mind" (nous) or better, "the pureness of heart" (*kardia*), which alone can penetrate the spiritual realm. The grand tools of that adventure are dispassion *(apatheia)*, which is the condition for gnosis and *theoria* or contemplation. The basis of true theology is holiness, not acumen. Recourse to God then requires grace that the Fathers understood to be uncreated—the uncreated energy (Greek) or operation of God (Latin). In other words, to "know" God and his character and will comes to us by divine action that involves, to repeat, the sanctification of human nature, which involves the saving or therapeutic truth, doctrine, by which the Church gives expression to her faith. The origin and apprehension of Christian truth is, of course, beyond reason; but to publicly defend it, it is sometimes necessary, and only with the greatest temerity, to verbalize and conceptualize the mysteries of God, to translate them into doctrinal formula. There is no elevation of faith into cognitive knowledge, no understanding of faith (*fides*) as assent without rational knowledge.

According to St. Hilary of Poitiers, the Church always hesitates to put into words divine teachings. "The errors of heretics and blasphemers force us to deal with unlawful matters, to scale perilous heights, to speak unutterable words, to trespass on forbidden ground. Faith out of silence to fulfill the commandments, worshipping the Father, reverencing with Him the Son, abound in the Holy Spirit, but we must strain the poor resources of our language to express thoughts too great for words. The error of others compels us to err in daring to embody in human terms the truths which ought to be hidden in the silent veneration of the heart" (*De Trin.* II, 2 PL 10 21A). So likewise, St. Dionysius the Areopagite says, "With wise silence do we honor the Inexpressible" (*Div. Nom.* 2 PG 3 589B).

THE NEW ATHEISTS

As we said before, to grasp this enigmatic truth requires the love of God rightly, existentially, as and to live the kind of life he wishes for us. To repeat, God "came forth" to reveal and realize his purpose in man. In love, God discloses himself to recover the creation from the devil and that his creatures might share his life. The Church Fathers use the noun "deification" (*theosis*) to describe the purpose of his Incarnation. In the words of St. Paul, "According to His purpose and grace, which was given in Christ Jesus before the world began, but is now made manifest by the appearing of our Savior, Jesus Christ who abolished death and has brought life and immortality" (2 Tim. 1:10). In the celebrated dictum of St. Athanasius of Alexandria, "God became man that man might become god." As Vladimir Lossky said, this is the soteriology "echoed by the Fathers and theologians of every age."[1]

In other terms, one person of the Holy Trinity became a man to eliminate those demonic forces that separated the human race from the Creator and to give man eternal life or participation in the divine nature by the uncreated energy of grace (2 Pet. 1:4). As St. Paul wrote, "Forasmuch then as His children are partakers of flesh and blood, He also Himself likewise took part in them; that though His death He might destroy him that had the power of death, that is, the devil; and deliver them who through fear of death were all their life in bondage" (Heb. 2:14–16). The idea of demonic evil seems to have disappeared from the "theology" of the secular West; even the Lord's Prayer is commonly recited "deliver us from evil" rather than "from the evil one" (*apo tou ponerou*).

On account of the silent postulate of the *analogia entis* or the notion of God and man sharing the same being (albeit graduated), the theologies of the post-patristic Western intellectual tradition have been unexpectedly diverse as Karl Barth reminds us. Such developments would not have occurred if the theology of the West had not followed the positive theology *(kataphatic)* of post-patristic "theologians" had followed the negative theology of the holy Fathers. If it had remained faithful to the wisdom of its Christian past, its philosophers and theologians would not have quarreled over the possibility of "natural theology" or presumed to systematize what a mystery is. In its attempts to define reality, Western thinkers produced deism, henotheism, polytheism, pantheism, or Unitarianism, yes, even atheism. Attempts to define him would have been avoided, and the accusations of his indifference to or even his inability to prevent or remove human suffering would not have been hurled at the advocates of Christianity.

It would be impossible to find many who appreciate that a "darkened reason" must necessarily impede our "knowledge" of the Maker. In modernity, surely, most have given little thought to the spiritual condition of man. Holding to the idea of man as a rational being, there is little attention to the idea that religious truth comes with virtue; and under these circumstances too, rationality functions at its level of design and, therefore, allows reason to encounter things transcendent. It is necessary to point out that St. Paul's declaration to the Romans, "That the invisible things of Him from the creation of the world, are clearly seen, being understood by the things that are made, even His eternal power and Godhead" must not be isolated from its moral context "because that, when they knew God, they glorified Him not as God, neither were they thankful; but became vain in their reasoning (*dialogismos*) and their foolish heart was darkened. Professing they to be wise, they became fools ..." Atheism and idolatry presupposes impiety, and it is from this conceit that gave rise to greater unrighteousness and, thus, to false understanding of God and, to be sure, atheism. Men had "changed the truth of God into a lie, and worshipped and served the creature more than the Creator, who is blessed forever. Amen" (Rom. 1:21–27).

There is nothing more critical to the modern philosophical enterprise than epistemology or theory of knowledge, at least since Descartes. It is the basis of every rational judgment. Once chief of all the atheists, Anthony Flew said, "The epistemological question is inescapable." The New Atheists have ignored the question of knowledge in their quest for a life without the "supernatural." They have arbitrarily chosen not to justify atheism in any form of epistemology. They are materialists, and therefore, knowledge demands only sense-data for "evidence." Reason acts according to what "the manifold of the senses" has provided. If so, such a position nullifies the root of their atheism. The New Atheists cannot "prove" the existence or nonexistence of anything spiritual, not only because all knowledge is assumed to be empirical, an assumption that cannot be proven from any philosophical or scientific position, but obviously because they despise the very notion of the supernatural as well.

Moreover, the late Professor Flew, having quoted Bertrand Russell ("perception gives no immediate knowledge of a physical object"), says, "If this were true ... then, there is no such thing as perception. And since the scientists do and must rely for the ultimate vindication of their discoveries upon direct observation, this conclusion undermines the findings from which it is derived. In short, this point of view removes the basis of all scientific inference."[2] The words of Professor Flew are clear. Modern philosophers and scientists have generally not seriously examined the epistemological qualifications for the possibility of knowledge. An indomitable problem occurs: the subject knows the object either directly (immediately) or indirectly (mediately). Idealism merges thought and its object, empiricism bifurcates them, and the "cleavage takes place in reality," blocking all lawful inferences concerning the truth that alone ought to be engendered by the rational process.[3] In other words, if the object is known immediately, there is no explanation for error; if it is known mediately, there is no certification of truth. The Four Horsemen or New Atheists have not taken the time to examine this argument and thereby throw the truth of their atheism into doubt. In a word, they must take it on faith.

It seems strange that most modern atheists have paid no attention to the demands of epistemology largely because they have never examined the epistemological aspects of their speculations and because most atheists (and evolutionists) hate philosophy. Nevertheless, most of these schools have taken the position, including Stephen Hawking, which was expostulated by Roger Scruton, the English philosopher who distinguishes, as he must, between subject and object or the physical object and our perception of it, laying our trust on mediate perception (*Modern Philosophy*, London, 1996, p. 333). How, for example, do atheistic evolutionists justify their "biological absolutism" when they have no certainty that what they perceive is a true image of the thing-in-itself?

The favorite philosopher of the New Atheists is David Hume (1711–1776). Charles Darwin cited him with great confidence, especially his *Dialogues Concerning Natural Religion*, a treatise against any rational (i.e., empirical) knowledge of God. Christopher Hitchens allotted him many pages in *The Portable Atheist: Essential Readings for the Nonbeliever*, completely oblivious to the implications of Hume's analysis of causality. Careful reading of Hume ought to grieve our New Atheists. As Bertrand Russell observed in his *The History of Western Philosophy* (New York, 1997, p. 674), Hume has proved "that pure empiricism is not sufficient basis for science." He made special reference to Hume's book, *An Enquiry Concerning Human Understanding* (1748), which offers a theory of knowledge that, in fact, the *Dialogues* presuppose.

Hume declares that the sine qua non of *knowledge* is causality—cause and effect. It cannot be empirically assured, he says, because the same cause cannot always and with theoretical certainty guarantee the same effect. Empiricists follow induction and, therefore, unless observed, can never be certain that, for example, a billiard ball striking another ball in the same way will always drop into the same pocket. It is not scientific to say that it will because it always has. This is custom or habit, not fact. There is no certainty that the sun will rise in the morning, not unless the phenomenon is observed. "The mind can never possibly find the effect in the same cause by the most accurate scrutiny and examination," he asserted. "For the effect is totally different from the cause and, consequently, can never be discovered" (*Enquiry*, sec. IV, pt. 2; sec. V pt. 1).

The New Atheist literature shows neither genuine comprehension of Hume's argument nor the insight of the French philosopher Gabriel Marcel (1889–1973) that the application of the principle of causality to God is the primary source of atheism. If they had studied the history of philosophy, the New Atheists would recognize that their devotion to science is subjective, say, better, a faith in science. Hence, knowledge is equated with scientific verifiability. Truth is nothing more. Necessarily then, science is the judge of all human experience, including religion. It is the same blindness that permits them to welcome Hume's belligerence toward "natural religion" while ostensibly espousing his epistemology. This bias undermines their entire defense of materialism and condemns Dawkins, Harris, etc., to live with an unresolved contradiction. A personal need for atheism seems to be the only reason for their adoption of it.

Sam Harris should have listened to his own words about "faith." "Belief, in the *epistemic* sense—that is, belief that aims at representing our knowledge about the world—requires that we believe a given proposition to be *true*, not merely what we wish were so."4 That our New Atheists have made no attempt to provide atheism with a metaphysical and epistemological framework proves, if nothing else, that they live by faith. Atheism is a brazen hypothesis, not the result of serious research. They will not test the viability of their theory, refusing to engage the real issues involved in the question of God's existence and the metaphysical implications of that existence, such as the origin and destiny of the cosmos whether it is, in fact, dual or monistic and, of course, whether the fabric of the universe is intelligible; and to be sure, what is human nature? Of course, they boast that their atheism is the outcome of rational (scientific) inquiry. It is almost ludicrous that atheists criticize religious people as stupid and superstitious because they have not fixed the ground beneath their own feet. But "the religious impulse" by which men live is, in fact, more credible than the New Atheist conviction that the totality of human experience may be traced to the chemistry of the brain.

The New Atheists deprecation of "faith" is undoubtedly another example of their parochial (Western) heritage. The nature of their unbelief is nothing new. Only their tactic is *new*. Again, they have not examined the phase "faith is assent without knowledge," which is a philosophical maxim, not a biblical or patristic axiom. Neither is the Christian understanding of "faith" commitment without evidence, for Christianity is a historical religion resting on facts and history that include reason. The facts abide within the memory of the historical religious community of the Church. Again, true faith takes human faculties to a higher level of cognition, something to which the New Atheists are oblivious. In addition, patristic reason has the advantage of grace, the Holy Spirit, something with which the New Atheists have not come to terms, also, medieval struggle between "faith" and "reason" of which the New Atheists have taken a position. In point of fact, there is nothing in the rumination of the Fathers that leads us to believe that "faith" and "reason" need to be reconciled or parallel or antithetical.

It would seem that Scholastics and their occidental heirs failed to recognize that there are several kinds of faith exercising reason in different ways. Thus, Cicero and Augustus Caesar differed in faith and, therefore, in their political philosophy were disparate. The faith of Aquinas was not the faith of Averroes. Consequently, their cosmologies differ. Luther's faith was not the faith of Pico della Mirandola, and therefore, they differed in their application of reason. The French revolutionaries and King Louis XVI did not share the same faith in God, and therefore, their understanding of government varied. There is no reconciliation between Christianity and evolution unless they have a common anthropology. Modernity will not escape nihilism unless it radically alters its rationalism. Perhaps to start, we should accept Lev Shestov's quip that "truth is spiritual and transcendent" and is apprehended with the "spiritual eyes everyone possesses and which so many have closed."

The man who thinks he can live by reason alone lives in "a state of fantasy." The post-patristic theology of the West evolved from an erroneous metaphysics and a "pride in reason." It is on this tradition that the New Atheists are feasting.

The word "supernatural" is part of a philosophical vocabulary that strictly differentiates between nature and grace, transcendence and immanence, and spirit and matter. Moreover, "natural theology" proudly makes no plea for special knowledge with its inquiry, nor does it call for reason's rehabilitation for man to encounter the deity. This "science" ignores in its formulations a world of the spirit that informs and sustains and will eventually transform the cosmos. Of course, rejecting the existence of the Creator God, any God, rationalists and materialists attack the question of God's existence. Probably never hearing of the uncreated energies or operations, those aspects of the divine nature by which he normally acts outside himself, the New

Atheists are confined to that theology with which they are familiar. Consequently, they have a false concept of God and his activity. Without the energies, the essence of God is active. They are therefore ignorant of who God is and what he does.

If New Atheists were aware of this history, their thinking might have taken a different direction, having lost the reasons for their unbelief. In part, it is this ignorance that gave them reasons for their atheism. Put another way, it is a rationalism that originates with the idea of God as being, the alchemy brewed in the synthesis of Christianity and Hellenism initiated by medieval philosophy. The Church Fathers, on the other hand, employed Greek philosophy as a means of discernment, not discovery. With regard to the "knowledge" of God, it is not by "the traditional arguments" that we learn of his existence. As the Spanish philosopher Miguel Unamuno said, these arguments "prove no more than the existence of this idea of God."5 St. John of Damascus tells us, "It is not within our capacity … to say anything about God or even to think of Him, beyond the things which have been divinely revealed to us, whether by word or by manifestation, by the divine oracles of the Old and New Testaments." As already implied, "The knowledge (gnosis) of God is implanted in us by nature." If it is missing in some, it is because "the wickedness of the evil one has prevailed so mightily against him so as to drive some into denying the Existence of God" (*De Fid. Orth.* I, 2–3, PG. 94 793BC). If St. John sometimes has recourse to philosophical argument, it is not *un acte de persuasion* but a contrivance to stir the divine embers of the soul on which that "knowledge" of the supernatural was originally stamped.

How then is God to be engaged? Speculation is futile. We need a total reconception of his existence, dismantling initially the notion that the knowledge of God is a philosophical proposition. He is neither an object nor an abstraction. We reach him spirit to spirit or, better, by preparing the "inward man" morally for their meeting. The major role is played by the "heart" (*kardia*), the source of love (agape), not *eros* or *amor*, that is to say, of good and evil and, consequently, the seat of the mind (nous). To start, the soul, at the center of which stands the heart, must be purged because the passions it contains are impediments to the divine-human engagement. As the Lord declared, "From out of the heart proceeds evil thoughts, murders, adulteries, fornications, thefts, false witness, blasphemies" (Luke 6:45); and "But those things which proceed out of the mouth come forth from the heart; and they defile the man" (Matt. 15:18). These are the corrupting passions (pride, lust, anger, etc.) that must be expunged if the wall between man ("the heart of man") and the Creator is to be removed. The passions must be expelled from the heart, and the heart must be guarded against their future incursions—under the auspices of the devil. In the admonition of Proverbs 2:23, "Guard (*Pase phylake*) your heart (*kardian*) more than anything else, because the source of your life flows from it." We must be able to recognize evil, the chief function of reason, fighting it with prayer, liturgical and private, and fasting. They who engage him, who "see" the true God, are the "pure in heart" (Matt. 5:8).

In the post-patristic West, the commonplace definition of the theologian is one who systematically examines the nature of God, along with church history and doctrines of religion. If we inspect the writings of the Fathers, there is considerable difference between their understanding of theology and what has developed in the West over the last millennium. According to the Fathers, Christian theology is the "knowledge" of the Trinitarian God with no reference to metaphysics or epistemology. It is a religious or a "mystical" experience, which is the privilege of those who have been initiated into the life of Christ through his Church. Only those who belong to him, however, may know him, love him, and engage and commune with him. No more than his own can become like him. Outside the Church, the knowledge of him is miniscule, even distorted; and therefore, intimate and salvific association with God is impossible whatever the attitude of those who seek him.

Thus, St. Gregory the Theologian writes, "Not to everyone, my friends, does it belong to philosophize6 about God, and not to every person. The subject is not so cheap and low; and I will add not before every audience, nor at all times, nor on all points, but only on certain occasions, before certain persons, and within limits." Moreover, "not to all men, because it is permitted only to those who have been examined and are passed masters in contemplation; and who have been previously purified in soul and body or, at least, are becoming purified. For the impure to touch the pure is unsafe, as looking with weak eyes into the rays of the sun" (*Theol. Ora.* XVII, 3). In particular, one must not discuss theology with anyone who is hostile to God or disinterested in the quest for him. They are neither repentant nor humble. Gregory, if he were among us, would not have been in favor of public debates with the New Atheists.

The "knowledge" of God is not acquired by ratiocination. "For what will we conceive the Deity to be, if you rely upon all the approximations of reason?" St. Gregory inquires, "Or to what will reason carry you, O most philosophical of men and best of theologians, who boast of your familiarity with the Unlimited?" He is nothing that can be imagined. If reason is to comprehend him, he would need to be "circumscribed." He is not and, therefore, not the object of thought. Consequently, such expressions as "when" and "after" and "before" and "from the beginning have no meaning" (*Theol. Ora.* XX, 3) and cannot be attributed to the incomprehensible deity, thus, the abrogation of the absurd question: "Then who made God?"

Who he is shall never be discovered; he only reveals himself. He is *deus absconditus*. He engages his creatures by his uncreated energies or operations or by his Logos or Incarnation. We may know him personally because as said before, he "enlightens every man that comes into the world." Some speak with "the spark of Divinity." We are urged to seek communion with Father, Son, and Holy Spirit and for this one needs the illumination of "the one God, One in diversity, diverse in Unity, wherein is a marvel" (*Theol. Ora.* XXVIII, 1). That we know him by revelation is to love him, "Who will have all men to be saved and to come unto the knowledge of the truth" (1 Tim. 2:4).

St. Gregory of Nyssa said the same. "But if one asks for an explanation or description of the Divine, we shall not deny that in such wisdom as this we are unlearned, for there is no way of comprehending the indefinable inasmuch as the Divine is too noble and too lofty to be indicated by a name: and we have learned to honor by silence that witch transcends all reason and thought" (*Contra.*

Eun. 2 PG. 45 601B). In the words of the Psalmist 139:6, "Such knowledge is too wonderful for me; it is high, I cannot attain to it."

St. Paul also draws our attention to a general revelation of God to man: the uncreated energies (Eph. 1:19, 3:7, 4:16; Col. 1:29; Phil. 3:21; 1 Thess. 2:13, etc.). The early Church Fathers mention them.[7] St. Pope Leo the Great exclaims, "By day or by night His voice is heard and the things of beauty made by the Operations of the one true God, a beauty that never fails to instruct the ears of the heart with the teachings of reason so that 'the invisible things of Him may be perceived by the things that are made'" (*Serm.* XIX, 2); and St. Basil the Great comments, "The Spirit is by nature unapproachable … but communicated only to the worthy; not shared in one measure, but distributing its Energy according to the portion of faith …" (*De Sp Sanct.* 22 PG. 32 108C–109A). There are innumerable energies or operations working through the divine persons. Grace and light are the most common to human experience.

St. Paul writes to St. Timothy that God alone "has immortality and dwells in unapproachable Light" (1 Tim. 6:16). It is the same light that shone on Christ as he stood on Mt. Tabor. The light was so great that the disciples could not look at him. As St. Gregory the Theologian said, "This is the Light of Divinity, saying that 'the Light of the divinity manifested to the disciples on the Mount'" (*Ora.* XL 6 PG. 36 365A). St. Basil the Great adds the Light of Tabor is "the beauty of Him Who is almighty, and His noetic and contemplatable divinity" (*On Psalm* 44, 5 PG. 29 400C). According to St. John Chrysostom, "The Lord appeared upon the mountain more radiant than Himself because the Divinity revealed its Glory".[8] The Light is the eternal light of God's Kingdom, "the beauty and resplendence of the divine Nature, the vision and delight of the saints in the age without end."[9] Thus, the Transfiguration of the Lord by the light on Mt. Tabor was the adumbration of eternity—the future was thrown into the past. The light is the superessential glory of God. It is the glory the saved will share in the age to come.

Uncreated light is not gifted to us by imitating Christ but through the action of God himself in and about us for reasons known only to Himself. Light and grace proceed from the essence and are both impersonal. The two dimensions of God are not identical. Grace transfigures human nature so that it might become godlike. As St. Maximus the Confessor affirms, "Salvation as deification is accomplished only by the Grace of God" (*Ambig.* 64 PG. 91 1389) via the redeeming work of Jesus Christ.[10] For those who dwell *en Christo*, in his risen body, the Church, the Holy Spirit is given or, more precisely, by the energy of the Spirit. We receive him according to the measure of our faith and dedication.

Christians need not ponder the origin of life or fabricate a theory to explain it. Creationists contend that thousands of years ago, God, the blessed Trinity, created both the physical universe and the spiritual dominion. He formed them in six periods or "days" or "ages." The New Atheists have nothing but evolution to explain the existence of the universe. Although all evolutionists are not atheists, all atheists are evolutionists. Most of the New Atheists hate Christianity and scorn evolutionists who are believers. Richard Dawkins makes no accommodation to Christian evolutionists whom he compares to the English Prime Minister, Neville Chamberlain, who believed compromise with Hitler was possible. He also attacks the evolutionist and philosopher Michael Ruse, teacher of the philosophy of science at Florida State University, for seeking an alliance with religious people who favor evolution.[11] Inasmuch as Dawkins holds that naturalism alone explains cosmic existence, his hatred for all religion is understandable. Indeed, it would seem that such accommodation is contrary to his philosophy.

Utterly repulsive to Dawkins, etc., is the idea that there is a Creator who accounts for the cosmos with its design and destiny, with man central to his economy. Abhorrent to him also is the idea that there was a first man, the crown of creation, brandishing free will to account for much of what is good and much of what will be evil in the world. The fall of Adam was the antitype of a "new creation," inaugurated by Christ and his Church. Furthermore, fallen and moral man was not denied the right to exercise his genius and to discover truths hidden in the tapestry of the created world. His ability derives from *imago Dei* (or starting point for the attaining the divine *likeness*). Dawkins and his comrades have no tolerance for the biblical anthropology. Of course, they have no answer for the origin of man, except to say that he has evolved over millions of years.

Yet there are some who find no necessary conflict between science and Christianity. The agnostic Stephen Jay Gould (1941–2002) hoped to protect religion and science by erecting two domains (*magisteria*) of thought. Each has "equal worth and necessary status for any complete human life ... they remain logically distinct and fully separate in styles of inquiry, however much and however tightly we must integrate the insights of both *magisterials* to build the rich and full view of life traditionally designated as wisdom."[12] He disagreed with Dawkins, who pontificates that omnivorous science "can make *probability* judgments on the subject" of God.[13]

Neither does he recognize the existence of spiritual truth that gives humanity access to things transcendent. Of course, there is some truth in Gould's words that religion and science should not compete for the same turf, but he falls short of a most fundamental verity—religion (and then surely, the religion of the Fathers) involves a different mentality from the "neutral" scientists whose province is confined to the understanding of the physical universe. So long as each remains within its own domain, there is no antagonism; but at the same time, science may not contradict revealed doctrine, while religion should not invade the province of science. In any case, science relies on reason for its "evidence" or stratagem, while Christianity, at least, has a special knowledge, gnosis, a distinct comprehension of the origin and purpose of things denied to reason.

In fact, the only struggle is between religious faith and secular faith or the dispute that the faith that descends from God and the faith man places in himself and his achievements, that is, the faith that promises participation in the divine nature and the faith that promises self-apotheosis. The reason of the first, empowered with grace, recognizes and defends mysteries; the reason of the secularist is hope of creating heaven on Earth. For the Fathers, reason (*dianoia*, ratio) has no function to span the spiritual realities it encounters. It is a lower part of the hierarchy of knowledge.

In his *Ascetical Homilies*, homilies 62 and 66, St. Isaac addresses this matter. There are three levels or degrees of knowledge. The first or "contra- natural knowledge" entertains things appertaining to the visible world and things appropriate to it, "such as arts and sciences …" The second degree involves thoughts and the desires of the soul, the quest for virtue, overcoming the passions. As "contra-natural knowledge, "It shows the heart the ways which lead to faith, and collects what is useful for the journey. But even here, knowledge is still related to what is material and multiple." Excellent as it may be, this knowledge does not bring us God-pleasing faith. The third degree of knowledge "is the degree of perfection." One who is caught up to this domain "comes to resemble the invisible powers." It is gnostic, the knowledge that "soars above earthly things and the cares of earthly activities" and that "begins though belonging to what is within and hidden from the eyes," possessing the grace that opens the way to "the mysteries that are concealed." It is beyond the scope of rational or empirical verification.

The "supranatural knowledge" or third kind of knowledge (gnosis), grounded in true faith, puts the believing soul in touch with the sphere of the spirit by faith and commitment or, in the words of St. Isaac, "That which dawns forth in the soul through divine Grace, and which, by the testimony of conscience, fortifies the heart, giving it the certainty of hope which is free from all doubt. This faith manifests itself not through increased hearing of the ears, but through spiritual eyes, which see the mysteries veiled in the soul, even that divine Treasure, which is hidden from the sons of the flesh…" This was the same experience enjoyed by the prophets, apostles, Evangelists, martyrs, and God-bearing Fathers. To them came the grace to grasp, articulate, and disclose the divine truths of their religion.

The New Atheists are not the only savants who think church doctrines are propositions. In fact, they are not logical premises or postulates or hypotheses. They are, as already mentioned, verbalized spiritual truths. They are revealed, not discovered. Even more, they are not directed only at the intellect. Contrary to our New Atheists, the "evidence" they want is not the "evidence" within the scope of scientific inquiry. Christian doctrine is not "falsifiable." It is not espoused because they satisfy the intellect but because they heal the soul. Spiritual truth is something beyond the telescope and microscope. It is the experience of the soul.

But there is greater evidence. To start, we may speak of the fall of man, which accounts for the "darkening of the nous" or mind as the result of the loss of communion with God.[14] God's plan is to restore human nature to spiritual health by the grace of truth, the grace found only in the Church, his body, the temple of the Holy Spirit, the life of the Sacraments, especially the Eucharist. Truth is more than a concept, more than a correspondence between thought and being. It is a mystery, a therapeutic force, involving prayer and fasting. Thus, dogmas are not written merely to make statements about what the Church believes, such as the Nicean Creed, but to stigmatize falsehood, to bear witness to the revealed truth, while healing the members of the Church that rightly believe. "Dogmas about God are ... towards illumination and glorification."[15]

For this reason, doctrines and creeds cannot be changed. In other words, dogma does not "blind" the believer; it cautions and guides his reason. We are submissive to the wonder, the antinomy of mystery by which the believing heart seeks union with the eternal. The divine truth and mystery will forever elude the atheist. It neither illumines nor heals him. They are also idolaters because they equate their own ideas and principles with the truth, including their conception of the philosophical God whom they disdain. As Fr. John Romanides said, "It is idolatry to identify God with some idea that we have about Him." It is idolatry when we "we think that our idea about God is God when we identify our idea with idea of God ..."[16] The end of true faith is deification: to be sinless, incorrupt, and immortal, participating in those truths that belong naturally to God.

The New Atheists take up the old argument that if there is a God, why is there evil and its concomitant suffering? Either he is unable to abrogate them or he will not. Thus, he is either impotent or malignant. If either answer is attributable to him, how can he exist? Their logic is ancient and faulty. There is no reason for God and evil not to coexist temporarily because evil needs God inasmuch as evil is the negation of the good. If God did not exist, evil could not exist, that is to say, evil signifies the existence of God, for evil is also the departure from good, from the "moral law" that implies the existence of a transcendent Lawgiver. Yet we cannot depend on this sort of argument to "prove" that God must exist. Although manifesting itself in human experience, evil, as the origin of goodness, is suprarational. In any case, some like Richard Dawkins have taken the arbitrary position that evil does not exist, and what men call evil is no more than something accidental and anomalous. Thus, if there is no evil or sin or right and wrong, with "goodness" and evil nothing more than something social and relative, his conclusions are as shallow as they are contradictory.

There is something very specific that the New Atheists despise about Christianity. Daniel C. Dennett is not the only atheist who finds objectionable her teaching concerning sin and hell. As all religions, he says she induces people to do good and avoid evil with the threat that they must be good or go to hell. There are several things wrong with this scenario, not the least of which is to think that God's mercy and justice "demeans human nature."[17] Unfortunately, Dennett is mistaken about human nature and the destiny of those who by their behavior have forged them. Sin is the cause of all the moral evil on an earth under the supervision of the evil one or Satan who, out of envy, endeavors to draw the human race to his side. The New Atheists think of God as a tyrant who uses fear to threaten and compel men to obedience. Heaven is the reward of the obsequious, and hell is the reward for the defiant. Contrary to the popular notions of the Hereafter, Heaven and Hell are not places to which God consigns his creatures. Each man or woman is responsible for his/her own fate.

Dr. Alexander Kalomiros makes this salient point. "God was slandered by theologians in the West … who presented Him as an eternal punisher and avenger." They made "God out to be the cause and creator of perdition, and they failed to properly attribute perdition to the creature, who misuses his freedom and to reject the God who loves them, choosing to isolates himself eternally in the perdition of his aloneness." It became ordinary in the West to blame an adamant God who went so far as to punish his Son on the Cross for our sins and cast those who do not accept the atonement, the disobedient, into "outer darkness." He seems "to be bound by a higher, blind impersonal necessity which forces Him to be Just." This idea of God grew and promoted the rejection of Christian Orthodoxy in the West and, "deep down, to the cause of contemporary atheism."[18]

It is a counterfeit theology that minimizes the notion of God's great love for his creatures. He has manifested that love in many ways aside from the Cross. It is time to ask: Why has not a dysfunctional nature (floods, earthquakes, tornados, etc.) demolished the human race? Why have not the innumerable wars in the twentieth century brought an end to humanity? Why has not everyone died of cancer? Why, despite the evil that men do, has the human genius produced immortal works of art, music, literature, poetry? For the atheists, there is no explanation, save the ad hoc genes and circumstance. The judgments of the intellect leave us unconvinced. Philosophers cannot help "wretched creatures who have killed their own spirits with their logic."[19] It is only the love and mercy of God, the same God who visits us in time of suffering, to console and teach us that by "the true faith," anguish brings wisdom and endurance. It is only God, as a person, who accounts for the value of a single human being. Remove him, nothing has any value. There would indeed be a "transvaluation of values." It is he who shows us how to repel the evil one and how to expel the demonic passions and the despair that comes with them. With the grace of Christ and the enlightenment (*photismos*) of the Holy Spirit, everything has purpose and draws us to the timeless God by whom and for whom we were made.

Whatever the truth about God, evil, and suffering, the fury of the New Atheists is not assuaged. Their unbelief came long before their hatred of the idea of hell or their abhorrence of the biblical God who allegedly erected it. Dawkins describes this Christian doctrine as the destiny of the unrepentant sinner, a place where he experiences "sulphurous smell of burning brimstone and the agonized screams of the forever damned."[20] In one of his famous quotes, he proclaims sardonically, "He will send us to hell to suffer forever and ever. That is really Amazing Grace!" He also eagerly cites Thomas Aquinas and Tertullian, who from their site in heaven joyfully watch the damned suffering in hell. Dawkins is not alone in the error that heaven and hell are places to which God assigns us. For this notion, he might have read Dante's *Divine Comedy*, which dramatically propagated the conventional Western belief that hell is everlasting agony.

In his classical "The River of Fire: A Reply to the Questions: Is God Really Good? Did God Create Hell?" Dr. Alexandre Kalomiros offers the traditional (patristic) understanding of hell. He introduces the subject with comments on atheism. He holds that atheism is not a real disbelief but rather an irrational aversion to God. Denying him is the atheist's revenge. But why do they hate him? In truth, their deeds are dark, while God is light. They fear the consequence of their errant lives. They think of him as a cruel and vengeful judge. The devil, Kalomiros contends, whispers this slander into our ears.

The devil has replaced the truth with a deception, deducing it from the Western dogma of salvation in which God has killed his Son to satisfy his pride. He spread his wrath upon his own Son that his divine majesty might be exalted. "The judicial conception of God, this completely distorted interpretation of God's justice, was nothing but the projection of human passions on theology," writes Dr. Kalomiros.[21] It begins with the falsehood that we should be grateful that he has saved anyone inasmuch as none deserves salvation as many Reformers proclaimed. From this soteriology, this separation of the righteous and the damned into separate categories, atheism was born. It hopes to negate this evil God. It was this very God against which so many people have rebelled. They wanted to kill him. Some say this is the meaning of Nietzsche's Madman, "God is dead!"—*Gott is tot!*

What kind of God is it that permits Adam's guilt to descend equally to all his children and that all are sentenced to death and damnation by the first's man's sin—"the original sin"? This is purely philosophical fabrication. It is wrong to teach that death was inflicted upon man by God. Adam fell into death by his free choice to disobey. He was warned by God not to eat of the tree of knowledge of good and evil, but he and his wife willfully disobeyed and were "driven out" of the Garden of Eden by a wrathful God. Contrary to this post-patristic soteriology, St. Anastasius the Sinaite reminds us, "We became mortal since we were born from a mortal person."

It was the Protestant Reformation that inadvertently but vigorously promoted this concept of a vindictive and arbitrary Deity, especially in the horrendous idea of predestination. For example, Calvin and Luther taught that we are saved by created grace alone; and therefore, sinful man has no choice in his salvation that belongs to the divine mercy alone. Predestination is the doctrine that God, in his secret and eternal council, capriciously chose to save some and condemn others. Roman Catholicism differs from Augustine and the Reformers in the belief that man has a free will and that the Almighty judges the sinner according to his deeds; nevertheless, the damned suffer the penal fire in hell, while the saved or the "elect" enjoy with their physical eyes the vision of the divine essence.

There is nothing in the Scriptures or the Fathers that lend credence to the idea that Gehenna or hell is a place created by God for the physical torture of humans administered by demons. According to Archbishop Lazar (Puhalo), who agrees with Kalomiros, the popular mythology of Hell is one of "the powerful dynamics in turning people away from God, and rejection of Christ."[22] What then is Hell? "This is Hell: everlasting exposure to the presence of the love and glory that has been rejected". The destiny of the damned is not separation from God but ever in his presence with his love and light or the "fire" that "burns" them.

It is a living death "where we find out the true nature of the worldly happiness we sought in the earthly life, and that it was really bondage to the passions that we were seeking, and now we have it, for all eternity ..."[23] Finally, it is medieval mythology that heaven and hell are created realities and that the damned will not be able to look upon God. In fact, they will see him, but his presence will be the source of their pain. St. Basil tells us that in the book of Daniel are the records of the three Hebrew men (Shadrach, Meshach, and Abednigo) who were unharmed by the fire of the furnace into which they were thrown, while the same fire burned and killed the servants of the king. To cite St. Isaac the Syrian (*Asc. Hom.* 28),

> *It would be improper to think that sinners in Gehenna are deprived of God's love. Love is the offspring of knowledge of the truth which is commonly confessed, is given to*

all. The power of love works in two ways: it torment's sinners, as happens when a friend suffers from a friend; but it becomes a source of joy for those have observed its duties. Thus, I say this is the torment of Gehenna: bitter regret. But inebriates the souls of the sons of heaven with its delectability.

In other words, those who suffer in hell are scourged by "the love of God, of His energies" (St. Gregory the Theologian). The Byzantine writer Euthymius Zigavinos observed, "He is the God who illuminates and brightens the pure and burns and obscures the unclean."

In other words, the reprobate and the righteous forge their own destinies. Their faith and behavior in this life determine their lives in the next. They who belong to God through their struggle with the passions, who fervently seek to unite with him, and who cling to "the faith once delivered to the saints" (Jude 3) will find reception in the Kingdom of God, while those who accommodate their passions; who vigorously pursue pleasure and power to live according to their own understanding of life and death, right and wrong; and who espoused a false creed will find a place in Gehenna. God does not by any "secret counsel in eternity" decide the end of his creatures. His mercy and justice are available to those whose own spiritual purpose is "according to His purpose" (Rom. 8:29).

It is noteworthy that the Fathers do not teach that after death, the souls of the saved must be purged of all their sins before entering paradise or heaven. There is no state of purgatory; rather, on the basis of Scripture and oral tradition, the Fathers delineate the adventure of the departed souls as the encounter with the angels, which carry them to the Particular Judgment—to hades, the abode of the dead—while the righteous enter paradise (or as the Lord promised the thief on the cross, "This day you shall be with me in Paradise") or Abraham's Bosom, the Hades of Light, as St. Hippolytus tells us; and the unrepentant go to "darkest hades." These states of the soul anticipate their final end.

At the same time, the prayers of the Church, even if only one of her members appeals to God for his mercy, interceding in behalf of the departed soul, may induce him to transfer it from "darkest hades" to paradise. Thus, it is said that St. Pope Gregory the Great saved the Roman emperor, Trajan, through his prayers. No influence is greater than his Mother, the angels, and the saints. Until Christ's Final Judgment when all things are decided, there is yet the hope of salvation for all. As St. Paul wrote, "He wants all men to be saved and come to the knowledge of the truth" (1 Tim. 2:4). The ridicule of atheists that God's plan for the redemption of the human race loses its bite in the face of the Christian eschatology, which they have never understood.

APPENDIX: Perhaps the strongest (if not the most common) reason for atheism is human suffering, especially that of children. This agonizing protestation of the human heart is nowhere better expressed than in Dostoyevsky's *The Brothers Karamazov*. There or anywhere else no argument, no evidence, to answer the old fulmination: God either cannot or will not purge the world of the ancient torment. But if God is omniscient and *omniabona*, how is it that he has not erased suffering from a world over which he has indisputable control and for which he claims to have such great love?

The most common response to this theology is the words of the Isaiah (58:3), "For my thoughts are not your thoughts, neither your ways my ways." In a word, there is no analogy between God and man that is precisely what the prophet insists. To his creatures, God may dispense by his uncreated grace and his incomparable goodness, justice, truth, and holiness. Too often, as already said, God is judged by the same morality he calls upon man to follow, such as the Ten Commandments. Necessarily then, if he ordered the Israelites to wholly destroy the Canaanites, the New Atheists condemned him as a "moral monster."

God cannot be judged: the Creator cannot be judged by the creature, especially if the difference between them is infinitely immeasurable. It is surely presumptuous to define his limitations particularly if we do not know what they are or if he has any. To judge him requires that we know him and that such knowledge is relevant to the argument. We have already said that such knowledge is impossible unless he is personal, and he reveals himself to the creature. And to be sure, he has not enlightened himself to everyone, only to those who are worthy as the Church Fathers tell us.

Yet the complaint will be that we do not know why he allows suffering even among the innocent, whatever his purpose. We do know because our knowledge is limited and, indeed, because his wisdom will not allow it. Let it not be asked why he does not notify us what or when it will happen. Such information may be forever beyond our ken. At the same time, we cannot forget that most children have not died of cancer, not all women have lost their babies stillborn, or not all soldiers have been killed in battle, etc. So much suffering has not happened that might have occurred. So much suffering has been prevented through prayer—the objections of Sam Harris notwithstanding. And of course, let us remember the suffering human beings have inflicted upon themselves and nature (floods, earthquakes, forest fires).

There is more to this matter that St. Paul tells us. "For I reckon that the suffering of this present time are not worthy to be compared with the glory which shall be revealed to us … For the creature was made subject to vanity, not willingly, but by reason of him who hath subjected the same in hope, because the creature itself also shall be delivered from the bondage of corruption into the glorious liberty of the children of God. For we know that the whole creation groans and travaileth in pain and together until now …" (Rom. 8:20–23). Man corrupts nature, and nature brings suffering on man. Man and nature are bound together. Sin and virtue, good and evil are inseparable inflicting suffering on the creation. Only the renovation of man will bring health on him and nature. But neither man nor nature can alter his being. Deny the one true God and his suffering will grow. It will continue to grow no matter the creative genius of humanity, not as punishment but because separation from the Creator separates man and, therefore, nature from his life. Only God is immortal and incorruptible. To unite with him is an act of free will. To reject him is an act of the passions.

CHAPTER III END NOTES:

1. St. Irenaeus, *Adv. Haer.* V, pref. PG. 7 1120; St. Athanasius, De *Incarn. Verbi Dei*, 54 PG. 25 192B; St. Gregory the Theologian, *Poem. Dogma* X, 5–9 p. 37 465A; St. Gregory of Nyssa, *Ora. Cat.* 25 PG. 45 65D; St. Maximus the Confessor. *Ad Thal.* 60 p. 90 921AB; St. Hippolytus of Rome, *Ref. Omni. Haer.* X 30; St. Cyprian of Carthage, *Tr.* VI, 15; St. Hilary of Poitiers, *De Trin.* X, 7; St. Ambrose of Milan, *De Virg.* I, iii 11 PL 16 202C; St. Jerome of Stridonium, *Contra Jov.* II, 29; St. Niceta of Remesiana, *De Sp. Sanc. Pot.*, 3, 4; St. Peter of Ravenna, *Serm.* LXVII PL 52 391AB; St. Leo the Great, *Serm.* XX, 5 PL 52 211C; *Hom. Proph. Ezek.*, I, i 14 PL 76 801D–802A.
2. *There Is a God: How the World's Most Notorious Atheist Changed His Mind.* New York, 2007, p. 37.
3. Berdyaev, N. *The Destiny of Man*, trans. N. Duddington. London, 1954, p. 2.
4. *The End of Faith*, pp. 61–62.
5. *The Tragic Sense of Life*, trans. J. C. E. Flitch. New York, 1954, p. 160.
6. The word "philosophize" is not to be confused with the more familiar term. It means rather to put into communicable language the results of contemplation.
7. See David Bradshaw's excellent *Aristotle East and West: Metaphysics and the Division of Christendom.* Cambridge, UK, 2006, pp. 119–152.
8. In St. Gregory Palamas, *Topics*, 146.
9. What the Fathers called the eighth day, the last and everlasting age that follows the seven ages of history and the Judgment. Sunday is a type of the "last age."
10. In the introduction to *Maximus Confessor: Selected Writings*, Jaroslav Pelikan writes that "it has been difficult for systematic theology to encompass (deification), as the fifteen centuries of the history of Augustinianism in the West, whether Roman Catholic or Protestant, more

than amply attest" (p. 11). The error here is double: (1) "Augustinianism" does not become dominant in the Orthodox West until at least the ninth century, and (2) all the Latin Fathers advocated deification by the uncreated energy (see my *Ye are Gods: Salvation According to the Latin Fathers* Dewdney, British Columbia, 2002).

11. *The God Delusion*, pp. 90–94.
12. *Rocks of Ages: Science and Religion in the Fullness of Life.* New York, 1999, pp. 58–59.
13. *The God Delusion*, p. 81. Sam Harris believes that religion is begotten of the "neural- circuits" (*The End of Faith*, pp. 50–51) that, of course, open its scientific investigation. Christopher Hitchens dedicates chapter 18 in *God Is Not Great* to this question. Daniel C. Dennett contends that "religion is in its death throes; today's outbursts of fervor and fanaticism are but a brief and awkward transition to a truly modern (scientific) society in which religion plays at most a ceremonial role" (*Breaking the Spell: Religion as a Natural Phenomenon.* New York, 2006, pp. 34–40).
14. Although expelled from a historical paradise, St. John of Damascus said the historical Adam and Eve were deprived of their "likeness" (likeness in virtue) to God, they he retained a dysfunctional "image" (mind and free will) (*De Fid.Orth.* II, 12).
15. Metropolitan Nafpaktos, *Empirical Dogmatics of the Orthodox Church According to the Spoken Teachings of Father John Romanides* (vol. 1): *Dogma-Ethics-Revelation*, trans. Mother Pelagia Selfe. Levadia, Greece, 2008, p. 190.
16. *Ibid.*, p. 259.
17. *Breaking the Spell*, p. 279.
18. *Nostalgia for Paradise: Guideposts on the Path to the True Fatherland and Through Our Life in Christ*, trans. G. S. Gabriel. Ridgewood, New Jersey, 2006, pp. 16–17.
19. *Ibid.*, 22.
20. *The God Delusion*, p. 359.

21. Third Appendix in Archbishop Lazar (Puhalo), *Gehenna: The Nature of Hell According to the Orthodox Christian Church*. Dewdney, British Columbia, 2012, p. 171.
22. *Gehenna*, pp. 7–8.
23. *Ibid.*, p. 25.

CHAPTER IV

NEW ATHEISM AND THE CHURCH

He believes in God who professes the Holy Church unto God.

—St. Peter Chrysologus

The New Atheists have no understanding of the Christian Church, an ignorance shared by not a few people. She is generally subsumed under the category of "religion." It is an ignorance born of indifference; and also, there has been an effort to redefine her and to accommodate a science, an ideology, and, therefore, Christology and history.

Obviously, there is no relevance to the old adage, "All religions may be wrong, but only one can be right." Clearly, if there is no God, a personal God, there is no revelation, no saving faith; and religion is best understood as "ultimate concern," to borrow Paul Tillich's phrase. It is the product of the human imagination. In point of fact, the New Atheist opposition is to supernatural religion (particularly, Christianity) has little in common with sacred nature of the Church. It would seem that the late Christopher Hitchens is right: it poisons everything.

Peering into the literature of the New Atheists, there is to be found only the dark side of the Church history reported. Always there is the jeering at the Crusades, the Spanish Inquisition, the Salem witch trials, etc., without the slightest concern for their religiopolitical, economic, or ethical implications. Inasmuch as there is no God, theology of any sort has no value. There is neither revealed nor natural religion; indeed, no distinction between true religion and idolatry, such as the Nazi devotion (*Gott mit uns* on belt buckle) and Eastern Orthodox. Their ignorance of the God and religion of the Old Testament—mined only for its ostensible contradictions and exaggerations and, therefore, the truth of atheism—is ample proof of the New Atheists' lack of objective scholarship and fairness.

Perhaps we can justify this accusation with an examination of the Christian religion. The Church is much more than the revelation of the true and perfect way to serve God in Jesus Christ, the Incarnate deity, the second person of the Holy Trinity, the Logos, "Who enlightens every man who comes into the world" (John 1:9). She constitutes a mystery "which from the beginning of the world has been hid in God" (Eph. 3:9). He came to unite all things visible and invisible. Therefore, "the Church is more desirable to God than the heavens," writes St. John Chrysostom. "He did not take on the body of the heavens, but the flesh of the Church." Therefore, "Nothing equals the Church" (*Exsil. Ante* 2 p. 52 429; *Occas. aut. Eut.* 1 p. 52 397). Thus, she is both the center of history and its entelechy. There will come a time when she will have become all that exists, the *pleroma*.

Why did God become incarnate? To recover the cosmos from the devil, who with his seduction of Adam and Eve become "the god of the age." By his death and resurrection, Christ deprived the devil of his sovereignty. Christ's plan (*Oikonomia*) was to become the "new beginning," the second Adam, as St. Paul observes. Adam was "the figure of Him that was to come" (Rom. 5:14). The Church then became the "second Eve." As his spouse, she became his body, the mother of the new humanity. Together, they form a new race opposed to "the race of Adam." If this be true, the Church is "a chosen generation, a royal priesthood, a holy nation a peculiar people."

The question becomes inasmuch all human beings find their origin in Adam, they must leave him for Christ through "adoption," that is, baptism, the mystery of incorporation into the body of Christ. None of this is found in the books or debates of the New Atheists. They hold with the popular Western idea of the atonement, that is, Christ was punished for our sins on the Cross. The Church Fathers and the early Church taught that he died on the Cross to destroy death and to recover the world from the devil and return it to God the Father. There is another aspect of this "mystery" too often forgotten. The Church is the spouse of Christ. Her members are the son and daughters of Chris, while he is "the first born of many brethren" (Rom. 8:29). Thus, if the Virgin Mary is his Mother, all his brethren are children of the Theotokos. No wonder St. Justin Martyr and St. Irenaeus, etc., referred to her as the second Eve. In other words, she is the Church; and inasmuch as we are saved through the Church, the reborn, the "new creatures" (2 Cor. 5:17) are saved through the Ever-Virgin Mary.

There are sound Christological reasons that the Mother of Jesus as a virgin begot him. As we have already mentioned, the common idea seems to be that her virginity was to protect him from the "original sin," which is transmitted by sex. The New Atheists are not alone in thinking the motive for the virgin birth (parthenogenesis) was abhorrence for sex. I have m not heard that they adopted the theory of Duns Scotus (1265–1308) that the Holy Spirit prohibited the delivery of the "original in" to virgin to prohibit its transference to the infant Christ. In truth, sex belongs to this life, whereas virginity belongs to the age to come, to paradise and heaven, where there will be no marriage and the propagation of the human race—"neither giving nor taking in marriage."

In fact, he was born virginally to initiate the Christian race— the Church. Sexual behavior has nothing to do with the Incarnation. There is no "original sin," the invention of Augustine's revision of the Christian anthropology. To repeat, the virginity of the Mother of God is to protect Christ from inherited mortality. Thus, if the Mother of God had borne the Savior in the ordinary way, Christ would have inherited death. As Adam was free to violate the will of

God, so Christ voluntarily chose to die on the Cross. Both Adam and Christ were born able to die, able not to die, to sin and not to sin. After the Resurrection, the Savior is unable to sin or die.

There are many other *types* of Christ; and the Church found in the OT or, in the words of St. Jerome, the NT is hidden in the OT, the OT is revealed in the NT. He refers to biblical typology, that is, historical parallels, thus, Adam/Christ, Moses/Israel and Christ/Church, Passover/Eucharist, Red Sea/baptism, Joshua/Jesus, etc. There are also antitypes, such as the disobedient Adam and the obedient Christ, and also the antitypes or negatives among the pagans, such as Horus and Dionysius, Attis and Krishna, etc., who were born of a virgin on December 25, died, and resurrected from the dead. They also had disciples. Such figures, even if mythological, are part of the divine preparation for the historical Incarnation—*praepratio evangelica*. We cannot forget that these antitypes made no claim that their messiahs were not the one true God. None of them had typified precursors. The difference between Christ and his pagan antitypes is that they contain theological aspects that differentiate them. For example, only Christ was transfigured by the divine light of God.

If St. Peter is right (1 Pet. 1:20, 3:10; 2 Pet. 2:5; Cf. Heb.11:7), there is no more important type than Noah and the universal flood. The New Atheists, as so many others, have no idea of their meaning. Some argue that this biblical episode is mythic and some that the Flood was not universal. The movies provide us with a vulgar version of this story. In truth, Noah and the Flood are historically authentic but not for the reasons ordinarily propounded. We ought not to be persuaded that this narrative is true only if science supplies the "evidence." Others insist that the infallible Scriptures must be taken literally. Both positions have some truth, but in fact, they both have missed the mark.

The ark is a type of the Church as Noah is the type of Christ. Noah and his family are eight, and the eight passengers are a symbol for eternity. They constitute an ending *(telos)* and a new beginning *(arche)*. In a word, the ark as Christ signifies the deliverance of the human race from destruction. Moreover, the Flood is universal as

THE NEW ATHEISTS

salvation is universal; but also, water is a type of baptism and the universal destruction of evil. Those who insist that the Flood was merely local hope to shield the scientific conclusions of evolution, which collapse if the Flood is historically accurate. In other words, deny the historicity of the ark, Noah, and the Flood and we deny the historicity of the salvific Christ, the Church, and baptism. Note the words of St. John Chrysostom:

> *The story of the flood is a mystery comprehended And the details are types of the future. The ark is the The Church, Noah is Christ; the dove the Holy Spirit, The olive branch is the divine Economy. As the Ark is in the midst of the waters protected those Within it, so does the Church protect those who Strayed ... (Hom. Laz. 6 PG. 48 1037–1038)*

In other words, typology is not allegory, that is, the use of symbols, art, poetry, or fictional beings to express divine and human realities. Christ was a historical figure, and the things that foretell his life and thought are themselves historical.

Christology and ecclesiology are likewise linked. Arianism rejected the divinity of Christ; therefore, the Church is purely human. Nestorianism separated the humanity and divinity of Christ, the latter flowing through former "like water through a pipe." In this case, the visible Church playing no direct role with our salvation, that is, deification. In addition, baptism fails to incorporate us into the body of Christ unless the historical community is equated with the body. For such heretics, the true and salvific Church is invisible "in the mind of God." In other words, the Christ of history cannot be the Incarnate God.

Christology gives us a view of time. Chalcedonian Christology tells us that time is a *coincidentia oppositorum*: the immutable eternity coincides with temporal history; in fact, they are linked "without separation or confusion," which explains, in part, the nature of the Church. There is no better explanation of this union than the divine Liturgy. It is a representation of the everlasting future. Nothing better explains this concept of time-eternity than the icon.

Thus, veneration of the icons passes to the deified persons, which it represents now dwelling in paradise. In other words, there is no clear division between "nature and grace" and no absolute bifurcation between things spiritual and things physical.

The intimate relation of eternity to time is evident with the presence of the divine light on Mt. Tabor. St. Gregory the Theologian (Nazianzus) referred to that light as "deity." It is the "unapproachable light" (1 Tim. 6:16) in which God dwells, that is, his glory, his uncreated energy. It was seen by St. Stephen, the first martyr. The Fathers clearly teach that this light is not created, and it is certainly not the essence of God. Thus, light, as grace and the other infinite number of uncreated energies or operations, of the three persons of the Trinity, act within time, creating, sustaining, and enlightening the cosmos. It may also be said that the light of God as seen on Mt. Tabor is a foretaste of the future, the glory in which the deified creature, reformed by uncreated grace, will dwell.

Insofar as the New Atheists are concerned, the major objection to the Christian historical philosophy is its lack of evidence, which the Scriptures, councils, and Fathers cannot provide. It is based on the supernatural that does not exist. And of course, evidence is always empirically achieved by the scientific method. In addition, religion depends on miracles without which there would be no Christianity, so we are told. Also, the Christian religion has proven itself false and contradictory in such matters as the Crusades or Inquisition as well as "original sin" and "the toxicity of sex," "legalistic morality," and syncretistic theology, all utterly "poisoned" by a tyrannical, puritanical, and intolerant biblical God.

As their scurrilous tomes attest, the New Atheists are not "religious" or historical scholars and philosophers and, to be sure, are not dedicated to the truth, which their relativistic idea of truth does not permit them to promote but which they never fail to do. The aim of their quest is for confirmation of their atheism, which they have laced with intolerance and animosity. Evidence for this accusation is their indifference to, as well as the ignorance of, the "theology" and "piety" of the Orthodox Church and her Church Fathers. Christopher Hitchens makes dismissive remarks about the

THE NEW ATHEISTS

Russian Orthodox Church but clearly shows that his knowledge of her church history is trivial. He also mocks the Church for calling on iconographers to paint icons of Joseph Stalin. I would like to know who gave him this information. What difference does he think it makes? In any case, the New Atheists castigate anything called Christian or theist even polytheist if it smacks of the supernatural. From reading their books and listening to their debates on the Internet, it is clear that they know nothing of the Church Fathers. They show some familiarity with Augustine of Hippo,[1] but we have no reason to believe that if they have read his books, it was not simply to fiddle with his thinking.

Also, it would have been of value to them to study what is commonly called the writings of the Church Fathers. With this boast, they might not have been accused of prejudice and lacking in the information that validates their boast of genuine scholarship. In any case, patristic thought is so much nonsense.

We have no reason to suppose that our self-satisfied Four Horsemen really care about the history and nature of religion. They are dilettantes. In addition, they have shown no concern for those who have warned us against the dangers of atheism. There is nothing in the writings of the New Atheists that leads us to believe that they have not taken seriously Albert Camus's avowal that atheism is "metaphysical rebellion" against God, a "rebellion" that has blossomed into the "terrible power of the state," into "a life of absurdity," even more to the contemplation of suicide. The atheist, Michel Foucault (1926–1984) thought so. Without God, there are no moral values; and without them, this life has no meaning. The absurd denies the existence of meaning for anything, including one's own existence. For the atheists, the idea of sin is repugnant and hateful because atheists have no such values. It presupposes ineradicable values and judgment. But more, any concession to the idea of sin and absolute values implies a verdict by history if not by a judge—God. They hold unreasonably that a designer or a Kosmokrator of the universe must necessarily arbitrate and control human thoughts and actions. But this capricious supposition has no evidence. Here is further proof that they know nothing about the Christian life that, among other things, involves the human soul, whose existence they deny from which God calls for humility and repentance.

We cannot be certain whether the New Atheists understand their choices or the implication of each. It is true, however, that the idea of sin and absolute values collapses the whole atheist scheme and, yes, the entire secularist enterprise that they have so publicly and passionately expostulated. With their dogmatic rejection of a personal God, designer, and judge, the New Atheists have nothing left to them but the formation of an anti-theist worldview. Whatever their protestations, they live by the faith that one day the world will welcome a godless paradise. The future will vindicate them. Their efforts to date proclaim that humanity will find a utopia based on a worldview composed of Darwinian and cultural Marxist principles. They have closed their eyes to the fact that there is no greater obstacle to their dream than the theory of knowledge.

The ambition of so many nineteenth-century savants was to justify their "metaphysical rebellion." How strange that they trusted in their method and purpose when with little more thought and honesty, they would have discovered that without a soul and without access to the spiritual world, the powers of reason can produce no theoretical certainty. No doubt they have invested all their hope in the wondrous successes of the physical sciences.

They might better have placed their confidence in men of wisdom, perhaps Christ; but that has been obviated by their doubt concerning his existence and, to be sure, by the palpable attempt of their nineteenth-century predecessors to deconstruct the doctrine of the Incarnation and all the historical claims made about the Savior.

That intelligentsia made every effort to prove that Jesus Christ was a mere man. He was not God, and he was not the Messiah. There is no better example than Ernst Renan's *Vie de Jesus* in which he wrote a life of Christ. He debunked the traditional image of him as a myth. And there were also Schweitzer, Reimarus, Paulus, Schleiermacher, Strauss, Baur, Wrede, Neander, etc., who went in quest of "the historical Jesus" and found none. Perhaps we should not invoke their names inasmuch as the New Atheists show us little that would incline us to believe that they studied their antecedents with care, if at all, Christopher Hitchens *The Portable Atheist* notwithstanding.

As so many before and after these corsairs, including the soi-disant "brights"—our New Atheists—atheists have shown no appreciation for the simple proposition that nothing is theoretically certain without a personal God, without his hand in the creation of man, a rational and noetic being, *imago Dei*. Thus, they naturally assumed that the Church's doctrine or dogma was of purely human construction, and they have no other recourse than to dismiss it as superstition. The alchemy of their logic has blocked all access to another way of thought, to another reality.

Not so the Fathers. Their engagement with the divine as well as their formulation of Christian dogma may not be compared with the experience of contemporary scientists and philosophers who depend on their hypothetical constructions for acquisition of truth. The source of patristic understanding is related to a reality of supralogical origin. The words employed in their verbalization of Church teachings are openly and admittedly inadequate expressions of divine truth. The patristic search for the right formula (*oros*) is not found in the agreement of thought with itself, observation of the senses, or "falsifiability" of the modern modus operandi and its results. The veracity of Christian dogma depends on the religious experience it presupposes, that is to say, the life of the Church or, to be more precisely, the enlightenment by the Holy Spirit that dwells in her (John 16:13).

There is no "evidence" that the New Atheists or anyone of the same mind-set have undertaken to authenticate scientific and philosophical conclusions, that is, to certify their metaphysics and epistemology. They have closed their minds to that responsibility. They are empiricists, and they have no choice but to define "knowledge" as wholly empirical. We have already seen St. Isaac the Syrian's diagnosis of *knowledge*. The New Atheists cannot refute his analysis even if they knew of it. Not even pragmatism will help them. They live by faith, the faith that the physical sciences will validate their mission.

There is another way. It was Jesus of Nazareth, the second Adam who inaugurated the recovery of what had been lost to the devil. With the Savior is the commencement of a "new creation," a new race of men. On "the *Tree* of the Cross," he defeated the usurper; and by his resurrection, the power of death was demolished. A new cosmic order was instituted. Christ became "the head of the body, the Church: who is the beginning, the firstborn from the dead" (Col. 1:18). Those who belong to him, incorporated into his body, are reborn through the Church, through her baptism, sharing in his victory over death and the devil, to the end that the ontological impediment to union with God has been abolished.

It is this soteriology that has been blighted by the post-Orthodox's West theory of the atonement. It is this theory to which the New Atheists are heir. It is this version of Christianity that they attack. They are also the victims of Augustine's doctrinal novelties, such as "original sin," predestination, and created and irresistible grace; and it was his eleventh-century disciple, Anselm of Canterbury, who concocted a feudal doctrine of the "substitutionary atonement," while those who subsequently followed him modified and confirmed the Anselmian soteriology, and it is this view of the redemption ("Christ punished on the Cross by His Father") that the New Atheists have excoriated as "theological trash."

They have no idea what they discovered even though they were able to trace some of it to Augustine of Hippo, who strengthened what later become known as the Western intellectual tradition. To be sure, the New Atheists were unaware that that it was cut off from "Eastern Orthodoxy" (of which they are deplorably ignorant) and, therefore, in their analysis of Christianity, were convinced that all versions were fundamentally the same. Furthermore, they had their own prevision of Earth's future. Either with Bertrand Russell, it would become an "ash," or with Karl Marx, the end of things is "beauty and freedom." I do not know if all the New Atheists are aware of philosopher Novalis's dictum: "What has always made the state a hell on earth has been precisely that man has attempted to make a heaven of it"—"*Was schon immer ein staat verruckt eine Hoelle auf Erden hat gerade, das man versuckt hat, um es in ein seinem Himmel.*" Of course,

THE NEW ATHEISTS

utopia has never been the objective of the Christian religion. The "new creature"—the deified universe is its destiny—the work of the Church and the Holy Spirit of God who dwells in her.

We need not wonder what the New Atheists would say to ecclesiology as cosmology. One may safely surmise that their reaction would be one of brazen skepticism. They have nothing but scorn for Christian exclusivism (or what is left of it), a predictable contempt for anything that bruises their egos, or perhaps hidden fear, the fear that in a world of probabilities, this one might be right. They shield their doubts with the bluster that "proud Christians" think themselves morally superior to the "worldly," no doubt an inference from their total misconception of the Christian eschatology. But as the Fathers teach, only true faith and humility are the promise of personal redemption.

Once more, the great Flood or cataclysm of Noah is a historical event; however, this may contradict Darwin's theory of evolution and the muddled "evidence" for the so-called Cambrian explosion. All the Fathers taught[2] that the Flood was not local but covered the entire earth to the highest hills as the book of Genesis records (Gen. 7:19–20). Richard Dawkins, however, holds that Noah's Flood was derived from the Babylonian myth of Uta-Napisthim (Epic of Gilgamesh) and acquired from the older mythologies of several cultures, perhaps the Akkadian and Assyrian, and "mythologies from all over the world, such as Hindu mythology of Matsya Avatar of Vishnu, the Puranas, the Deucalion of Greek mythology, the Mayan peoples of Central America, the Muisca people of South America, etc. Furthermore, the acerbic Professor Dawkins muses about this 'charming' legend about animals going into the ark two by two." "God took a dim view of humans, so he (with the exception of one family) drowned the lot of them including children and also, animals as well."[4] Why animals? So that the entire cosmos will be recovered from the devil and returned to God.

The destruction of the earth by the universal flood was the result of "the wickedness of man." God saw that it was "so great that in every imagination of the thoughts of man's heart was only evil continually. And it repented the Lord that had made man on the earth and it grieved him at his heart. And the Lord said, I will destroy man whom I have created from the face of the earth; both man, and beast, and creeping things; and the fowls of the air ..." (Gen. 6:5–7). It amuses Dawkins, etc., that the authors of Genesis did not devise a better reason for the annihilation of all living things. But then God was sculpted by the New Atheists as "a moral monster." They have not the slightest idea of the goodness of God or the sinfulness of men, especially their own. Evil is repulsive to God, and his "repentance" in having created wicked man is a sufficient reason for the eradication of Noah's world. But judging by their "moral code," our atheists will not grant the author of life his right to eradicate his work and to reconstruct it.

Unknown to them also, the Flood has another meaning, not allegorical but typological, that is, historical events in the Old Testament pointing to another in the New Testament, the first, "shadow," the second, "reality." St. Peter writes that God saved Noah, "the eighth person, a preacher of righteousness, bringing in the flood upon the world of the ungodly" (2 Pet. 2:5). In patristic exegesis, this and other like passages are a typology of the Church and baptism. The two are intrinsically related. The explanation of St. Justin Martyr is comprehensive:

> *In the Deluge was accomplished the mystery of man's Salvation. Noah the just, with the other men of the Deluge, that is, his wife, his three sons and their wives, formed the number eight, and so showed the symbol of the eighth Day (Sunday) on which Christ appeared risen from the dead. And which is always, as it were implicitly, day one (of creation). For Christ, the first-born of all creation, became in a new sense the head of another race, of that which was regenerated by Him, by the water and the wood? which contained the mystery of the Cross, as Noah was saved by the wood of the Ark when he was carried on the waters with his family. When, therefore, the prophet says, "In the time of Noah I saved you," as I have said already, he also spoke to the people of God, to the people who possess these symbols ... As the whole earth, according to the Scriptures, was flooded, it*

> *obviously was not to the earth that God spoke, but to the people who obeyed Him when He prepared for them a place of rest in Jerusalem, as He showed beforehand by all the symbols of the time of the Deluge; and I mean those who are prepared by the water, the wood and who repented of their sins, they shall escape the Judgment of God.* (*Dial.*188, 2–3)

The Flood is also a type of baptism that is both destructive and life-giving. In terms of the Noah drama, it is destruction of the ancient world and the beginning of another even as Christ is a new beginning of a new world with Noah and his family, "it is the herald of righteousness when He brought a flood upon the world of the impious … for the Lord knows how to deliver the God-fearing from temptation" (2 Pet. 2:4–9). The number 8 (Noah, his wife, three sons, and their wives) signifies the "eighth day," the day after the Sabbath (symbol of the "seventh day" or the last period of historical time). "Eight" is also Sunday or the day of the Lord, an earnest of the "eighth day."

But all these prefigurements of baptism points to the rebirth of the new man in the Church (the ark) and shares now in the age to come. In other words, he already has stepped into the "the eighth day" and already participates in Christ's Resurrection, which itself anticipates the universal resurrection and the inception of the age to come.

With good reason, St. Cyril of Jerusalem explains, "Some say that, just as salvation came in the time of Noah by the wood and the water, and there was the beginning of a new creation, and as the dove came back to Noah in the evening with an olive branch, so they say, the Holy Spirit came down on the true Noah, the Author of the new creation, when the spiritual dove came down upon Him at His baptism to show that He it is Who, by the wood of the Cross, confers salvation on believers and Who, toward the evening, by His earth, gave the world the Grace of salvation" (*Catech.* PG. 33 982B).

The wood of the ark is not only a type of the Cross but also adumbrates the Church. St. John Chrysostom says, "The narrative of the Deluge is a mystery and its details are a type of things to come.

The Ark is the Church; Noah is Christ, the dove, the Holy Spirit, the olive branch the divine goodness. As in the midst of the see, the Ark protected those who were inside, so the Church saves those who are spared. But the Ark only protected only a few, the Church does more." For example, the ark took in animals but not without reason. This type indicates that God will save the whole creation, not just men. As a type of the ark, the Church protects and transforms all that God has made, the people it welcomes (*Hom. Laz.* 6 PG. 48 1037–1038).

To summarize, the Flood, the ark, Noah, and his family promise salvation through the waters of baptism, the Church, which is the security of salvation or eternal life in the eighth day or the Kingdom of heaven. And yes, there is the implication as St. Cyprian exclaims, "If, at the time of this baptism of the world (the Flood) in which it was purified and redeemed, anyone could have been saved outside the Ark of Noah, then, he who without Baptism and therefore outside the Church can be saved" (*Ep.* 68, 2). Without baptism, there is no access to the Eucharist or what St. Ignatius of Antioch called the medicine of immortality.

The Old Testament gives us further typologies central to patristic ecclesiology—the Mystery or Sacrament of the Eucharist, sometimes called the mystical supper. There are many types in the Old Testament (Melchizedek, manna, Solomon's banquet, Jonah and the Whale, etc.) but none as vivid as Moses, Israel, Pharaoh and Egypt, and the Paschal Lamb. Moses is the type of Christ, Israel the type of the Church, Pharaoh the type of Satan, Egypt the type of the world, and the lamb the type of the Eucharist. St. Cyril of Jerusalem explains their relationship:

> *You must know that the symbol of the renunciation of Satan is found in ancient history. Indeed, when Pharaoh, that harsh and cruel tyrant, oppressed the free and noble Hebrew people, God sent Moses to free them from slavery to the Egyptians. The doorposts were anointed with the Blood of the Lamb, so that the Destroyer might pass over the houses that had the sign of the Blood. Let us go now from these ancient things to new ones, from the type to*

the reality. There we have Moses sent by God into Egypt; here we have Christ sent by the Father into the world. There the Blood of the lamb wards off the Destroyer; here to rescue men tyrannized in the world by sin; there the Blood prevents the Destroyer; here the Blood of the true Lamb, Jesus Christ puts the demons to flight. (ib., 33 1068A)

The blood is derived from the Paschal Lamb from which the people of Israel at in commemoration of the night in which they were freed from Egypt. Eating from the spring lamb and unleavened bread, the Hebrews formed a single nation as Eucharist forms the Church. With this, we come to understand the exclamation of St. John the Baptizer when he saw Christ: "Behold, the Lamb of God" (John 1:29).

In *The End of Faith*, Sam Harris prefers to ridicule rather than to understand the biblical typologies. He inscrutably turns our attention away from this exegesis to the philosophical concept of "transubstantiation" (i.e., converting the *substance* of bread and wine into the substance of Christ, while the accidents [color, odor, shape, etc.] of the bread and wine remain unchanged). I fear that Aquinas and the Scholastics invited this derision with their "explanation" of the Eucharist. Then Harris manages to add the irrelevancy that the same Lateran Council (1252), which had instituted this "incredible doctrine," also sanctioned the torture of Jews.[(5)] The council's understanding of the Eucharist was pushed aside to condemn the failures of religion. Furthermore, he does not even attempt to understand the relevance of the Eucharist or Paschal meal to salvation. Nothing in Harris's books (and the other "Horsemen") show the slightest curiosity concerning the slaying of the Passover Lamb and the application of its blood to the doorposts of Hebrew homes (Ex. 12:11–13), which foretells the death of Christ in which members of his Church are saved through the Eucharist, "the mystical Supper."

St. Cyril makes this point clear. "The communion in the 'chewing' of the holy Body and drinking the saving Blood contains the confession of the Passion (the suffering and death of the '*Lamb of God*' [Jn. 1:29]) and the freedom from death for us by Christ's death, as He said Himself in establishing this Mystery: 'Whenever you eat this bread and drink this chalice, you announce the death of the Lord.' In the present world then by Communion in these realities, we announce His death, and when we are in the glory of the Father, we shall no longer to confess His Passion, but contemplate Him purely, as God 'face to face'" (*ib.* 49, 428C).[6] This is the destiny of those who receive the body and blood of Christ with sincerity and dedication. He dwells in them even now. It is, in fact, sharing in future when the elect will be united to Christ and his saints forever. The Liturgy brings together inexplicably the "Church triumphant." As St. Pope Gregory the Great *(Dialogos)* says, the "two lives of the Church are one," that is, her visible and invisible dimensions are united "without separation or confusion," a metaphysic that has been forgotten in the West for a thousand years.

That unity is explicated by the icon. Its veneration passes from the icon to its archetype whether Christ, the Mother of God, the angels, or the saints. This is a manifestation of that unity by the icon: eternity seeps into time through it. The icon signifies the Incarnation in which God became man, showing once more the link between time and eternity. The icon is the promise of man's transformation, his deification (*theosis*). That soteriology is dramatized in the Liturgy, which itself is an "earnest" and further confirmation that the Church, his body and spouse, is already what she will become, the Kingdom of God.

"The Church is a mystery" as Fr. Georges Florovsky once observed. With all the elements that form her, there is curiously not a single patristic treatise on ecclesiology. What we know of her is typological or analogical. Surely, the Eucharist only deepens the mystery, especially when we consider that we literally foretaste our salvation, participation in the divine nature by grace, through the body and blood of Christ. It creates the union among her earthly members and between them and the children of God in paradise. Paradise is not purgatory but the expectancy of heaven when human nature and the cosmos will be transfigured or deified. Further silence is given to the Eucharist, which is fundamental to soteriological process. Thus, the Fathers give no explanation (St. Gregory of

Nyssa uses the innocent word "change") for the transformation of the bread and wine into the body and blood of Christ, a "change" that is performed by the Holy Spirit (epiclesis), which, a doctrine universally held until the Latin Middle Ages, was a divine action occurring everywhere in the liturgies or the Church. One thing is unambiguous: the Church and the New Atheists do not live in the same reality. We are about to see how utterly oblivious "the Four Horsemen" are to revealed religion.

The New Atheists could not survive in the reality described by the Fathers of the Church. The difference between them is radical, involving not only the cosmology but also their very approach to "the problem of evil." It is an occidental habit to treat God and evil and Epicurus's trilemma ("Is God willing to prevent evil, etc.") as something affirmed or refuted intellectually. What cannot be solved logically is reduced to a metaphor or a mystery to be deciphered later. In fact, evil is "supernatural," an antinomy of reason when it ought to be understood as belonging to another level of understanding. Not without some irony, the New Atheists have an answer to evil but only by redefining or denying it as Dawkins does. As naturalists, materialists, and monists, he and his associates cannot possibly have an answer. There is nothing in their metaphysics that permits a metaphysical solution.

There is natural and moral evil. From a Christian point of view, the latter presupposes the former, that is, the disobedience of our first parents. Hitchens or Harris or Dawkins, etc., take the position that "moral evil" is the consequence of social and economic inequities. What else could they do but agree with Rousseau that society creates poverty, sickness, war, crime, etc. The New Atheists cannot allow moral evil to be ontological. This too may be one reason that they are "cultural Marxists," where no guilt is attached to any moral indiscretion. They do not display any familiarity with the writings of Frankfurt School with its "critical theory" ("change the world do not interpret it"), but without a personal God, their ethical choices are limited and unverifiable. But then we cannot be sure that the New Atheists have probed the idea that this school is an ally.

Whatever the atheistic "ethic" may be, they do not know that it may eventually become a tyranny or that nihilism will infest their future. I have yet to read that the New Atheist delineate evil, moral, and physical in metaphysical terms. They seem to have the optimism that science will eventually resolve all such "problems." Behind such optimism is the assumption that reason as intertwined with the idea of human domination of nature, the singular avenue to theoretical certainty and pristine reality. They also think that nihilism can be overcome by developing a scientific vision of the good life.

The Scriptures tell us that physical evil is the result of nature's disorder with the introduction of death and sin through the fall of man or, in the words of St. Paul, "For we know that the whole creation groans and travails in pain until now" (Rom. 8:22). In truth, since man's expulsion from paradise and nature's corruption, there is nothing "natural," not even reason. On this account, the New Atheist's speculations about a golden age, perhaps a new paradise via science, will fail. They do not take into consideration the evil that infests humans thought and will. The world is filled with dreamers.

Christians realistically hold that the ultimate source of moral evil is beyond the competence of reason and its instrumentalities to explain or elucidate. It is not God, but it has personal cause. No doubt the New Atheists have heard the story of the pre-historical rebellion of the angel Lucifer to overthrow the monarchy of God. Cast into the realm of the first cosmos—seven levels were created—the devil and his demonic horde tormented the human race. He spread the illusion of his dominance among men by his lies and temptations. Of course, moral evil is the result of man's abuse of his free will but not without the influence of "the rulers of darkness, spiritual wickedness in high places" (Eph. 6:12).

Of course, Sam Harris and his cohorts view Judeo-Christian demonology as pure superstition directly related to "the Genesis myth," where Adam and Eve were deceived by the "snake" (devil) who prompted their initial disobedience. Whatever history is attached to this incident, there is more to it than melodrama. It declares that time and history are the arena of the cosmic battle between God and his insidious adversaries. It is the superficiality of atheist ruminations that causes them to deny that the cosmos is drenched in mystery, supernatural mystery. In a word, it is a mystery before which the syllogism is powerless, the philosopher is perplexed, and the scientist is muzzled. To be sure, science may one day explain the physical causes of flood or earthquake and volcanic eruption and, to some degree, restrain them. Dismissing such things, the New Atheists have placed all their *faith* in something to which they have contributed very little.

The nineteenth-century metaphysics of which Darwinian evolution is part, that is, the ontology of becoming vis-à-vis the frigid ontology of being in which not only man but also the cosmos evolves. Marx was an advocate, and his cosmogony is indebted to the absolute idealism of George Hegel. Although a monist, the latter's monism is spiritual. Hegel argued that all things emerge from the absolute to which they are preordained to return; hence, cosmology is cosmogony. Here is the "invisible hand" behind evil, that is, the absence of perfection or better, the distance of a thing from its end. It is the same ontology, albeit a materialist metamorphosis, the one that the New Atheists cosmology presupposes. Since the New Atheists are Darwinists and neo-Darwinists, they clearly fall within the scope of this metaphysics. It is almost amusing to hurl in the face of our atheists that their moral criticisms of Christianity and religion are nothing more than a Western heritage that has taken the form of "cultural Marxism."

The patristic cosmogony has nothing in common with this or any other form of rationalism and naturalism although, viewed from an ontological point of view, admits a reality both spiritual and material, being and becoming—*coincidentia oppositorum*—united without confusion. It is a truth of revelation as recorded in Genesis that the formation and design of the universe is the work of the omnipotent Creator. He has formed a mono-dual reality, related so that the one does not exist without the other. The spiritual world contains "intelligible and incorporeal essences."[7] The New Atheists are evolutionists who read the world, where they can, through the eyes of relativity and the ten types of quantum mechanics. This is a rigid concept of time and space governed by unalterable laws, while the Christian or patristic cosmology recognizes that the future reaches into the past, such as the uncreated light of Mt. Tabor and of the saints.

In addition, God intervenes at moments of his choosing to direct affairs beyond the ability or imagination of man to discern. Communion with omnipresent God and the admission to the spiritual realm is possible to men according to their spiritual condition. To be more precise, access to things spiritual, beneficent, and malignant depends on our relationship to God or the lack thereof. There is no more manifest way to engage the divine and escape "the wolf of the soul" than through the Mysteries or Sacraments (*sacramenta futuri*). The greater our allegiance to Christ, to the life he has given us to follow, the greater our freedom from the passions, the greater our acquisition of the Holy Spirit, and indeed, the greater our freedom— genuine freedom.

St. Basil the Great once called monks (*monochos* = male, *monoche* = female) "the most authentic Christians." St. John of the Ladder referred to them as the light of men. Daniel C. Dennett prefers to characterize them as "those contemplative monks who devote most of their waking hours to the purification of their souls and the rest to the maintenance of the contemplative lifestyle to which they have become accustomed. In what way, exactly, are they morally superior to people who devote their lives to improving their stamp collections or golf swing? It seems to me the best that can be said for them is that they manage to stay out of trouble, which is not nothing."[8] One would not expect an atheist could say anything else about "maximal Christianity." They must roll their eyes when they hear that monks go into the desert to combat the evil one in his lair. Dennett and his fellows cannot fathom how anyone could believe that the prayers of monks on Mount Athos did more to win WWII than all the bullets and bombs of the Allied armies and that the litanies of the monks of St. Catherine's Monastery have done more to drive all the sickness out of the world than the contributions to the breast cancer crusades or drug rehab centers.

The New Atheists are not alone in their ignorance of the Fathers and not alone in a hardwired mentality that refuses to appreciate their wisdom. They have not the slightest comprehension of individuals whose lives are a living repudiation of their worldview. The monastery straddles the line between time and eternity. The whole purpose of the monks is not only to live in future glory now but also to fill the universe with the grace of God. As far as possible, they want to achieve their destinies now. Here is the reason for the vows of chastity, poverty, and obedience. Their worship and discipline draw the Holy Spirit into their lives and the lives of other men and women into a foretaste of eternity. What brings the monk to this condition is the overthrow of the passions. In other terms, male and female monks yield their lives to what is holy and not the fear marriage or the detestation of sex or, what is the same thing, a loathing of the body. They surrender the legitimate pleasures of this life not because they are "toxic" but because they are earthly.

The Church honors holy virginity because it is angelic, heavenly, the state of the immortal. It is for this reason too that she holds the Mother of God (Theotokos) in the highest esteem; and yes, because she is the Church, that is to say, as the Mother of Christ, "who is the first-born of many brethren" (Rom. 9:29), she is our mother as Christ is our brother. From the divine services of the Orthodox Church, we hear:

> *It is truly meet to bless thee, O Theotokos, Ever blessed and most pure, the Mother of Our God. More honorable than the Cherubim And incomparably more glorious than the Seraphim, thee who without corruption (mortality) gave birth to God the Word, thee do we magnify?*

Of all the New Atheists, none is more certain than Christopher Hitchens that the Church abhors sex because it is "dirty," hence, the exaltation of virginity, that is to say, the body is evil; and presumably, marriage is the same. But the "flesh" is part of the resurrection and the consummation when the Church, the body of Christ, shall fill the cosmos, "the fullness of Him that fills all in all" (Eph. 1:23).

Others, more scholarly antagonists of Christian monasticism and its attitude toward sexuality, theorize that its historical roots are found in Neoplatonism. Whoever comes to this conclusion is not without a historical agenda. Scholarship that fails to distinguish between the transcendentalism of monasticism and the philosophical "mysticism" or pantheism of Neoplatonism needs to examine the existential matrix of both monastic and philosophical life. Plotinus, who hated his own body, was an idealist, the product of rationalism. He desired resurrection not in the body but from the body, while Christian monasticism is the quest for union with the one true God by grace in the body.

The return to God begins with the purification of the body from the passions and thereby frees the soul from its encroachments. As St. Anthony the Great states, "Evil comes from the passions found in matter, and so it is not possible for a body to come into being free from evil. The noetic soul strives to liberate itself from this evil-burdened matter; and when it is free it comes to know the God of all ..."[9] This is not contempt for the body but for its passions that, inasmuch as body and soul are united, may corrupt the body and pollute the soul. If God allows us to endure the ordeal of the passions, remarks St. Peter of Damascus, it is to chastise the sinner and thereby to save his soul.[10]

The monastic is aware that the first victim of the passions is the "heart" (*kardia*) through the agitation of the senses, "which coddles the flesh in order to foster its desires." Diseased by the passions," writes St. Gregory Palamas, the individual becomes "vain in his reasoning" and "out of the foolishness of their hearts (Rom. 1:21) form a world that does not exist" (*Topic*, 3); in fact, the mind that is alienated from God becomes either bestial or demoniacal. How then can we learn with certainty anything about God, his existence, or character? Our thoughts are fragmented, in turmoil, and deceived by dreams and the fantasies of the imagination, in a word, manipulated and constrained by the fallen self. The return to "normalcy" is the elimination of inward discord that is possible only by the quest for God and the eventual union with him through the Holy Spirit. The result, says St. Nikitas Stithatos, is "the wisdom-engendering intellections of the Divine" (*On Spiritual Knowledge*, 18; *Philokalia* IV). The questing mind gradually receives the primordial light that, as it draws near, purifies the soul and sets the mind on the path to

THE NEW ATHEISTS

divine union through heavenly wisdom and gnosis and to a world of indescribable things and eventually to oneness with God, a oneness in his uncreated energies, not the pantheistic identity of the deity and the creation as St. Basil the Great exclaims (*Ep.* 234, 1 PG. 32 869AB).

This astonishing experience takes much effort, eluding all those persons and things that lead to fatal distractions. In the words of St. Maximus the Confessor, "One keeps his soul uncontaminated for God as he strives to direct his mind to think on God alone and in his own virtues" (*Chapters on Knowledge*, 14). It is this dedication that leads people to think that monks are egotistical. The accusation is false until one acquaints himself with the ascetical experience. Although seeking another time, another place, the monk is not indifferent to his earthly duties—to feed the poor, liberate the prostitute, provide homes for orphans and the elderly, and even work in the monastery fields and vineyards. They have saved the Church from iconoclasm, Islam, the Latin Crusades, Protestant proselytizing, the Turkish rule (*turkokratia*), and socialism. They have been the Church's apologists, polemicists, iconographers, poets, hymnographers, and translators. In other words, the monk is the model for all Christians, that is, the one who "lose his life in order to save it." Nevertheless, self-abasement is the duty of all followers of Christ. The difference between the monk and the ordinary Christian is a matter of degree. They are both aware of the words of Christ to the rich young man, "If you would be perfect, go sell what you have, give it to the poor, and you will have treasures in heaven; come and follow me" (Matt. 19:21).

The essential practice of patristic Christianity is worship, the divine Liturgy, the mystery of the Eucharist. In particular, it is the pedagogue of her doctrine, the true and sincere holding of which is the precondition for participation in the mysteries or Sacraments of the Church. The Liturgy (Mass) is the dramatic elaboration or ritualization of her *weltanschauung* whose *sine qua non* is the true glorification (*orthos - doxa*) of God.

When the Sunday Liturgy is celebrated, the worship of the Church enters another theater of existence: present and future merge, for Sunday is "the image or icon of the Eighth Day"; and if it is a

Paschal Liturgy past, present, and future coalesce, the Resurrection of the Lord and the resurrection of the elect is anticipated. It is a mystical experience, the spiritual kingdom rushes into history. There will come a moment when all created things visible and invisible having passed through seven ages of history will cross the threshold of time-space into the endless stream of divine Infinity. It is for that reason that the Liturgy begins, "Blessed is the Kingdom of the Father and the Son and the Holy Spirit, now and ever and unto the ages of ages." The corporate worship of the one true God commences, present is the whole Church, the *Theotokos*, the nine orders of angels, the Fathers, the martyrs, the confessors, and all the saints as well as the inhabitants of paradise and the living. At the same time, it is the earnest of nature's restoration to its original normalcy for which reason the Church uses palms, flowers, incense, etc. These are the symbols of the transfiguration of the cosmos.

To exemplify the new condition of the saved, the resurrected unto eternal life, the faithful worships standing on Sunday.[11] St. Basil the Great tells us,

> *We make our prayers standing on the first day of the week, but not everyone knows the reason for it. It is not only because we are risen with Christ and that we should seek the things which are above, or that on the day of the resurrection we recall the grace that has been given us by standing to pray; but also, I think, because this day is in some way the image (eikon) of the future age. This is why also, being the origin (arche) of days, it is not called the "first" by Moses, but "one." "There was," he says, "an evening and a morning, one (mia) day," as though it returned regularly upon itself. This is why it is at once one and eighth (ogdoe) that which is truly one and really eighth, of which the Psalmist speaks in the titles of certain Psalms, signifying by this the state that will follow the ages, the day without end, the other aeon which will have neither evening nor succession, nor cessation, nor old age. It is, then, by virtue of an authoritative claim that the Church teaches her children to say their prayers standing on this day, so that, by the*

perpetual recalling of eternal life, we may not neglect the means which leads us to it. (De Sp. Sanc. 27)

This text constitutes a valuable witness to Orthodox historiosophy but also explains why we are forbidden to kneel on Sunday. The Sunday Liturgy as the image of the age to come, the eighth day, the last and everlasting day, the day when man is deified, death vanquished, sins abolished, hence, where there is no repentance and obeisance, which kneeling represents.

St. Gregory of Nyssa asserts that "Day One" and the eighth day are the same; the former is the beginning of all things and the latter their end, but both first and the last are the same, from eternity to eternity, from God and back to God—*vom Gott zum Gott*. He created the world in a week of days (whatever their length may be), history drawn to a close on the seventh, the Sabbath. The creation, the "week of days" or "ages," is a replica of the seven "ages" or "periods" of history (whatever their length may be). At present, history has reached the seventh age, the age of the temporal Church, the time after which begins the endless eighth day.

With the eighth day will come the complete revelation of the Christian Mystery for which reason at the Easter or Paschal Liturgy, all the doors or curtains of the iconostasis are opened. The sanctuary that was dark, covered in black altar clothes and curtains for Holy Week, but with the forty days Paschal celebration, the sanctuary is covered in white (glory). He who had been immolated Friday on the Cross is now risen, a rising in which our own rising is pledged. The devil overwhelmed, death has been conquered, sins forgiven, the way to Kingdom of the heavens inaugurated.

The purpose of the Lord's Supper ("mystical supper") becomes discernible. To unite with God and all his elect through participation in the body and the blood of Christ, a communion prefigured between God and the people of ancient Israel. In Egypt, they were protected against the angel of death, the new People of God from the death of reprobation. The priest prays, "That they (body and blood) may be to those who partake for the purification of soul, for the remission of sins, for the communion of the Holy Spirit, for the fulfillment of the Kingdom of Heaven ..."(12)

Before the reception of "the Gifts" (Eucharist), the congregation recites the Nicean Creed ("I believe in one God ..."), implying that the communicant holds the true faith, sine qua non to participation in the Sacraments, and professes it as the faith of the Church as well as him/herself. Later, the congregation as the "children of God" utters the Lord's Prayer, confessing that God is their Lord. "For as many are led by the Spirit of God, they are the sons of God. For you have not received the spirit of bondage again to fear, but you have received the Spirit of adoption, whereby we cry, Abba, Father" (Rom. 8:14–15). Communicants are one in Christ, or more precisely, the Church is becoming that unity through the body and blood of the Savior.

In him, the Church is offered to the Father in the sacrifice, also, because the All-Holy *(panagia)*, Mother of God, is the Church, for Christ is our brother, for brothers have a common mother, the Ever-Virgin Mary *(aei-parthenos)*. Having received the Holy Spirit twice, Incarnation and Pentecost, it is through her also that the "children of God" receive him. We also share in her personal piety as her children, the brethren of her Son. "The Mother of God united her mind to God by inner attention and unceasing prayer," St. Gregory Palamas informs us, "and by rising above the multiform jumble of thoughts and the senses, above every kind of image. Hence, she opened a new door to heaven where she, filled with the infusion of divine Grace, beholds the Glory of God" (*Topics* 68).

Such ideas would fatigue the Four Horsemen whose interest in Christianity is her folly, that is, a motive to ridicule theism itself, which surely includes as an object of derision any panegyric to the Virgin Mary. They have decided that the Church needed to invent this "legend" and whatever else attaches to the supernatural to feed the blank and feeble minds of her members. I have yet to experience or read what might be their reaction to her as "the new Eve," the mother of the new mankind reborn in Christ, the new Adam. The first Adam was born of virginal soil, Jesus of a virgin mother.

If Christ were born of a virgin, it was that his birth would mark the beginning of a new order or, in the words of St. Irenaeus of

Lyons, *in novissimus temporibus nove effusus est in nos* (*Adv. Haer.* IV, xxxiii, 15 PG. 7 1083A). Also, her virginity marks the beginning of a new humanity and, thus, the hymnody (*axion estin,* "It is truly meet …") honoring her after Christ as the greatest among all humans. The Church cannot be understood without her. She is central to ecclesial unity; indeed, she is the new Eve, the mother of the new humanity, Church. She is the Church.

The Eucharist is the Sacrament of unity, the unity of both "the quick and the dead." The way the Church manifests the presence of her children in paradise [13] during the Liturgy is the icon. The Lord, the Mother of God, the angels, the Saints, and all the departed worship together in the earthly Liturgy (*communio sanctorum*) or the shadow of eternity. The icon is not a mere religious painting; it is the visible ectype of its prototype with the latter mystically present in the former. It is flat to indicate the perimeters of reason and the senses. Only gnosis allows the sanctified believer to pass beyond the borders of visual representation of the painted figure on the icon. Again, the honor or veneration (*proskynesis*) paid to the icon passes to the original or prototype. This relationship intimates the union of the finite and the infinite, the visible and the invisible. It is also access to the eighth day from where the grace of salvation is poured.

Interesting too is the comparison with Roman Catholic iconology, that is, the porcelain three-dimension statue. It models Latin doctrine of "the superadded gifts" that were lost with the fall of Adam and Eve. Humans are perfect as they were in Eden, save that they lost the "superadded gifts" (*dona superadditum*), such as immortality, moral rectitude, etc. They have been returned to those in Christ. Perfection comes "from above" by created grace. Thus, the Roman Catholic flat halo that hovers over the head of Christ, the Virgin, and the saints indicates that sanctification descends "from above," while the patristic icons show the uncreated light emerging from within the sanctified persons to circle the head. Furthermore, Protestants employ no icons or statues in their worship. They are generally interpreted as idols, and the distinction between "worship" and "veneration" is dismissed as "hair- splitting" (John Calvin).

Having attended the Orthodox Liturgy with his Greek wife (1881–1889), whether Christopher Hitchens captured these themes, his books and articles do not reveal. There are some reports that he enjoyed the experience. It may be that his priest welcomed his attendance as an opportunity to convert him; he obviously failed. Yet Liturgy is a Sacrament of the Church, not an evangelic tool. Neither is the beauty of the worship meant to be an enticement for tourists, a spot for field trips, ecumenist curiosity, etc.

The divine Liturgy or the Church's other services are not open to public inspection.[14] It is the privilege of those who share the same faith—"the law of faith is the law of worship." Pertinent are the words of St. Dionysius the Areopagite: "But see to it that you do not betray the holy of holies. Let your respect for the things of the hidden God be shown in knowledge (gnosis) that comes from the mind (nous) and is unseen. Keep these things of God unshared and undefiled from the uninitiated (unbaptized). Let your sharing of things sacred befit sacred things: let it be by sacred enlightenment for sacred persons only" (*Eccl. Hier.* 1.1 PG. 3 372A). Prayers bring together in common faith those who come together for that purpose. [15] Most surely, the law of belief is the law of worship.

One may safely infer that such rigorous ecclesial praxis would not endear the Orthodox Church to the New Atheists. Christian exclusivism rests on the simple principle that there is only one baptism, one faith, and one acceptable worship pleasing to him. If this is true, is a Christian pluralism possible? One body is one Church, one Spirit pilots and preserves her in the truth, and one baptism presupposes one body and one faith. There is no reason to believe that God is a "God of confusion" (1 Cor. 14:33) who would reveal different beliefs to different people. He would be guilty of causing sectarian vertigo. Is doctrinal truth necessary for salvation? If we believe the book of Ephesians (4:4), then we cannot deny that doctrinal truth is mandatory precisely because it was ordained by God in Christ by the Holy Spirit. For that reason, the apostolic faith, despite the efforts of some to assimilate her to the secular culture, has endured unchanged. Thus, the faith was delivered by Christ to the apostles to become the yeast of all cultures.

THE NEW ATHEISTS

If the divinely revealed truth is compromised or lost, salvation is lost, the Church has no immutable tradition upon which her people may depend. There is no reason then to believe that Christ is risen, and if "Christ be not risen your faith is in vain, you are yet in your sins" (1 Cor. 15:17). In other words, if the New Atheist centered their attacks upon Christianity through a denial of the Resurrection, despite the strong and immense evidence for it, they would not need to strike so furiously against "the God of Abraham, Isaac and Jacob," for the heart of the Christian message is the Resurrection. There would be little reason for Dawkins to assail the Bible as "not systematically evil but just plain weird, as you would expect of a chaotically cobbled-together anthology of disjointed documents, composed revised, translated distorted ... by hundreds of anonymous authors, editors and copyists ... spanning nine centuries."[16]

His strategy discloses his aim. As the other New Atheists, Dawkins is not in quest of a philosophical or scientific refutation of Judeo-Christian theism but the spewing of their hatred, which is not always made known to their audiences. If refutation was their purpose, they would have relied on "evidence," not invective and mockery. To scholarship, Dawkins, etc., prefer "substituting turbocharged rhetoric and highly selective manipulation of the facts, with little scientific analysis, loaded with Pseudoscientific speculation, linked with wider cultural criticisms of religion, mostly borrowed from older atheist writings." Dawkins "preaches to his god-hating choirs," "who relish his rhetorical salvoes."[17]

Yet it may be that the New Atheists have deduced that if there is one personal God, there must be only one true Church. But not unexpectedly, they hold that Christianity is a multiplicity of numerous conflicting sects, each boasting that they possess the true faith. There is such an unholy reformation of the Church here that the New Atheists have presumed to restructure her, that is, break up the Church into numerous sects, each claiming to "the true Church" with the result that conflict leads to confusion, confusion to doubt, and doubt to rejection. Neither can the "true Church" be invisible, her members known only to God, lest her invisibility reflect upon Christ's Incarnation. Alter Christ and the Church is altered and vice versa. Finally, such confusion and skepticism would throw into question the testimony of Church's history and her Fathers. There must be one true way necessary to man's salvation, lest within a chaos of rival doctrine, nothing can be determined, nothing rightly worshipped. Perhaps we have given the New Atheists too much credit if we say they are doing the devil's business.

In any case, it is too late now for Dawkins and his friends to reshape their philosophical stance without throwing their atheism into serious doubt. They can make no concession to religious belief, no admission that it contains the slightest truth. There can be nothing special in the teachings of Christ; and there can be no Holy Spirit, no infallible doctrine, and no God-pleasing lifestyle. Distorting Christian history and doctrine is how they began, and it is the way they must continue. But then the Four Horsemen have never had any understanding of the Church and her nature and message.

Undoubtedly, Dawkins, Hitchens, Harris, Dennett, etc., will not care to take any aspect of Christian life and thought seriously. Yet a little truth on this matter may be useful to those who have honest interest in such matters, things. The New Atheists have proven more than once that they have no knowledge of Christian ecclesiology. For an accurate picture of the Christian doctrine of the Church, let us turn to *The Church Is One* by the famous Russian Orthodox, lay theologian-philosopher, Alexei Stepanovich Khomiakov (1804–1860). He says that all the "notes" of the Church are recognized only by herself and by those whom grace has called to be her members. "To those, indeed, who are alien from her, and are not called to her, they are unintelligible; for such as these, outward change of rite appears to be a change in the Spirit Himself, which is glorified in the rite ..." (*op cit.*, p. 1).

The devoted members of the Church, once exposed to her truth, the saving truth delivered by the Holy Spirit, possess an inward knowledge of faith, of its purity and immutability. Wherefore the Church has not been or could be changed or her faith obscured or could she fall away, for she is the abode of the Spirit of truth. There could never have been a time when she could have taken error into her bosom or when the people, the presbyters, the bishops would submit to instructions or teachings antithetical to the Gospel of Christ. She is his life among us. She is temple of his Spirit. It is he who guarantees the cohesion and survivability of the Church. A mystery, she cannot be conceptualized. The spiritual integrity of her life and doctrine is continually protected by the God the Spirit. She is both eternal and historical, united without confusion or separation, a reality nowhere better expressed than in the divine Liturgy.

There is no other way to explain why her faith has not been corroded over the centuries, and the purity of her doctrine retained *in toto*. Numerous modern church historians have written that a religion that would not change must eventually evaporate because she refuses to conform to "the spirit of the times." But the grace of God has preserved her until now, and he will not fail to protect her in the future. She can never lose her sanctity. "And where would there be truth if her judgments of today were contrary to those of yesterday?" inquired Khomiakov. "Within the Church, that is to say, within her members, false doctrine may be engendered, but then the infected members fall away, constituting a heterodoxy or schism, and no longer defile the sanctity of the Church."[18]

There is no other way. If the Church were divided into various sects, the truth would be hidden from or lost to her children. But the Church can no more be divided than the robe of Christ. In the words of St. Symeon the New Theologian,[19]

> *With love we pass on to you what we have received from the Fathers. We offer you nothing new, but only that which has been delivered to us. We have changed nothing and retained everything, such as the creed which remains in the in which it was given to us. We teach exactly as Christ Himself, as the Apostles and the Fathers did.*

The Four Horsemen have not adopted the thought of Dostoyevsky that human beings have three choices: one undivided God-redeeming Church, socialism, or suicide. Camus and Foucault gave serious consideration to the latter. One has the right to wonder whether our atheists have thoroughly studied these options. One of them has taken up the challenge. Victor Stenger prefers "infinite nothingness" to "dreadful superstition, such as the fear of hell ... in fact, I represent it to myself mathematically." It is not a choice born of serious examination but of pride. With Sam Harris, he thinks that "blind faith" is "the source of much of the unreason in the world. and a prime contributor to the terrorism and fanaticism we have experienced in recent years." None of the New Atheists are willing to distinguish between the faithful believer and the renegade, between the devotion and hypocrisy, nor have they given the slightest consideration to the idea that there is one true religion, while others, claiming to be a "branch" of the Church, have welcomed doctrinal innovation as a new revelation. Disparity between Christians is the result of departure from tradition.

An ecclesiology that allows for doctrinal diversity in the Church of God, dividing her into numerous sects, has already announced the existence of a false God, for as St. Basil the Great says (Canon I), the difference between Christianity and heterodoxy is a difference in gods. There is nothing more irrelevant than the complaint that "traditionalists" are seeking "to force medieval ideas on the rest of society."[20] Stenger seems not only uninformed about the number of "medieval ideas" he has exchanged for his scientific idolatry, but he also has closed his eyes to the "evidence" that favors Christianity and theism in general. In the New Atheist public proclamations, there is no reason to believe they have read with objectivity Christian literature or have familiarized themselves with any of its authors.

It is not the source of amazement then that the opposition of the New Atheists to the existence of God is "spectacularly weak," if we may borrow a phrase from Richard Dawkins. They have yet to undertake a justification of their naturalistic metaphysics or their positivist epistemology. They have not the slightest acquaintance with the idea that God will be found by only those who seek him and that replies come to those who search with "repentance and tears." The "knowledge of God" cannot be divorced from piety or, indeed, that piety is developed only with the struggle against the demons. And yes, it is impossible to join the battle without a belief in the spiritual world infested by them.

As evidence of this assertion, one should consider the observation of R. A. Varghese: "they refuse to engage the real issues involved in the question of God's existence." None of them have addressed the philosophical issues central to the understanding of reality, not only its constitution but also the means of contacting it. What is the origin of rationality, of its autonomy, of human consciousness, of human autonomy, of our consciousness, and of the self and its powers?[21] Varghese might had added that the New Atheists have not "engaged the real issues" because matter in motion does not constitute reality and, also, that the truth might not come solely from an individual but that a sacred community might be its custodian, including a knowledge of man's worst enemy.

The Church of the Fathers includes the apostolic tradition that encompasses the Scriptures ("written tradition"), the councils, the Liturgy, the sacred canons and customs of the Church, and the Christian asceticism. Again, there is a good reason that the decrees of the councils of the Church begin with the words "Following the holy Fathers." They speak for the whole Church or, in the words of St. Theodore the Studite, "For the confirmation of what has been said, it is necessary for it to be verified by patristic testimony" (*Antir.*, II, 18 PG. 99 364A). They are undoubtedly the chief diagnosticians of tradition and, therefore, the supreme exegetes of the Scriptures that, not so incidentally, are not the only source of Revelation.[22]

The Church and her tradition, her life, and her thought are so filled with the Holy Spirit that the revealed truth could just as well as have been communicated orally without fixing it in writing, such as Scriptures. Indeed, the truth would not have been absent if there were no Old and New Testaments at all. Revelation comes to her by the Holy Spirit, and his delivery of the saving truth is not confined to the written word. There is no greater channel of his will than the holy Fathers. Nevertheless, the Scriptures are held in special esteem, and nothing may be taught by the Church that contradicts them.

The apostolic tradition is nowhere better preserved, no more comprehensively and dramatically exhibited than in the divine Liturgy—*lex credendi, lex orandi*. It is the summation of tradition if only because she unites the two lives of the Church, her life in time and her life in eternity, which are united "without confusion or separation." The Liturgy foreshadows the everlasting age to come, the Kingdom of Heaven. Aside from the numerous citations from the Scriptures, the hymnology is dominated by the compositions of the Fathers. This church music is unlike anything familiar to the New Atheists if, indeed, they have made any contact with religious aestheticism at all. It is a certainty that they have no knowledge of that tradition, which the Fathers are the headwaters.

This tradition is the embodiment of a worldview, which is an unknown challenge to the atheist mind-set. It is a journey to communion with the one true God. It follows that tradition is a milieu, an experience of the Kingdom, not an authority, not a record of theological speculation, not the preservation of ancient documents. It is the "memory" of a new humanity, the Church. Tradition is a dimension of her collective life *(sobornost)*. In this life, the believer finds something not only whole but also suggestive of immortality, of something that points beyond itself. The future comes by encounter with the Spirit of the true God who dwells in her and manifests himself in the tradition of the one, holy, catholic, and apostolic Church.

I suspect that if the New Atheists had confronted this spring of forgotten dreams, they might at least suspect that they had been tussling with concepts and principles, especially the idea of God (theism) and a faith (Church), which did not represent the mind (*phronema*) of authentic Christianity, and that there might be other "religious paradigms" with which they ought to familiarize themselves. Perhaps if they were honorable, if lovers of the truth, they would inquire…

Commonplace is the objection that there is no unassailable doctrine inasmuch as it changes with time and circumstance, the doctrinal differences among Roman Catholic, Lutherans, Calvinists, Methodists, etc. How else do we explain the disparity between the conservative and liberal Protestantism? Then of course, there is the claim of the Orthodox Church that her faith is immutable. Her doctrine is unassailable, altered neither by circumstance nor human ingenuity. Normally, anything changes inasmuch it is subject human error and the demands of time.

In the case of the Church, however, her faith is protected by the Holy Spirit. Her faith, the truth, is the promise of salvation; thus, she offers "the faith once delivered (traditioned) to the saints" (Jude 3). It may be formulated by her councils and Fathers who have receive her tradition from the apostles. In the words of the second-century Father, Irenaeus of Lyon, "The tradition of the Apostles exists in the Church to this day." The Scriptures are evidence of this. The apostles are followers of Jesus Christ in whom the truth abides. This truth is transferred to those who learned directly from the apostles. Their disciples (e.g., St. Polycarp of Smyrna and St. Ignatius of Antioch) are the recipients of what was handed down in the Church (*Adv. Haer.* I, ii, 3; I, iii,4).

CHAPTER IV END NOTES:

1. *The God Delusion*, pp. 285–286.
2. The Fathers held that the Flood covered the entire Earth even to fifteen cubits above the highest mountains. See Gen. 7:19–23; St. Justin Martyr, *Trypho*, 138; St. Theophilus of Antioch, *Apol. To Autoly* III, 18–19; St. Gregory the Theologian, *Theol. Or.*, XXVIII, 18; St. John Chrysostom, *Hom. on Gen.* XXV, 10; 2 Pet. 3:3–7.
3. "I will ransom them from the power of the grave; I will redeem them from death: O death, I will be thy plagues; O grave, I will be thy destruction: repentance shall be hid from mine eyes" (Hosea 13:14). Christ died on the Cross not as a sinner but as a warrior. The Protestant "justification by faith" or right standing with God is achieved through the merits of the death of Christ, which is contrary to the Biblical-patristic doctrine, that is, participating in his victory via incorporation into his body, the Church. Her children have been ransomed from death and the devil (cf. Rom. 6). The result of *Christus victor* is more than a new status before God; rather, it forms a new nature or *theosis*,

that is, immortality that is associated with divinity; it is "the fruit of divinity" (see my *Ye Are Gods: Salvation According to the Latin Fathers*. Dewdney, British Columbia, 2002).
4. *The God Delusion*, p. 269.
5. *The End of Faith*, pp. 99–100.
6. This is not the Roman Catholic beatific vision but, looking upon the deified Christ, God the Son.
7. St. Maximus the Confessor, *The Church's Mystagogy*, ch. 2.
8. *Breaking the Spell*, p. 306. He includes Buddhist monks in this castigation of monasticism.
9. "A Work Attributed to St. Anthony," *Philokalia* (vol. 1), 50.
10. Introduction: A Treasury of Divine Knowledge, *Philokalia* (vol. III).
11. Until the thirteenth century, the West also stood during liturgical worship.
12. Anaphora of Liturgy of St. John Chrysostom.
13. Until the return of Christ, the departed souls of the saved enter paradise or Abraham's bosom. As the Lord said from the thief next to him, "Today you shall be with me in Paradise" (Luke 23:43), while the reprobate souls enter "darkest hades." The Orthodox Church calls this Particular Judgment. It is not a form of purgatory.
14. See Council of Laodicea, canon 6; Apostolic canons 45, 65; St. Theophilus, canon 7. Also, see 2 Cor. 6:14–17.
15. See A. Kalomiros. *Against False Union*, trans. G. Gabriel. Boston, Massachusetts, 1967. See 2 Cor. 6:14–18.
16. *The God Delusion*, p. 268.
17. Alistair and Joanna Collicutt McGrath. *The Dawkins Delusion: Atheist Fundamentalism and the Denial of the Divine*. Downers Grove, 2007, pp. 11–12.
18. *The Church Is One*. Liberty, Tennessee, 2000, pp. 11–13.
19. Quoted in J. J. Stamoolis, ed., *Three Views: On Eastern Orthodoxy and Evangelicalism*. Grand Rapids, Michigan, 2004, p. 242.
20. *The New Atheism*, pp. 27–28.

21. Introduction to Antony Flew, *There Is a God*, xvii.
22. See St. Basil the Great, *De Sp. Sanct.*, X, 25, XXVII, 66; and St. Vincent of Lerins, *Comm.* II, 3; XVII, 44, XXIII, 53–59.

Chapter V

The Quest

1I watched with interest the You Tube debates between atheists and the theist. Of course, the latter supported his position with the classical Western arguments for the Existence of the Deity --- Aquinas, Anselm, Leibnitz and, of course, Descartes. Both the atheists and the theists (past and present) assumed that God was BEING. Both parties formed their arguments in preparation --- if they could ---- for his opponent's response. They both began with the same idea of God, the one to affirm, the other to deny. Interestingly, they both initiated and elaborated their arguments from reason. Given their common culture, they could not find another way to prove their own positions or refute the position of his antagonist. Their presuppotions are regularly ignored.

If God is Being, then, He is subject to philosophical manipulation, none of which offers a necessary result. In any case, the Christian God is not "being," but "beyond being" (*hyperousios*) --- Roman Catholic or Protestant theology notwithstanding. The latter are grateful to Hellenism for the Being they claim is the Deity. I wonder if Pascal understood this distinction when he wrote, "He is not the God the philosophers and the savants, but the God of Abraham, Isaac and Jacob." I am not convinced that he conceived the Christian theologian as like Moses rather than Augustine. In any case, the atheists and the theists were debating the wrong God. They should read the Church Fathers ---- without the assistance of Western metaphysical categories.

There was not member of the dispute that included Christ as something intrinsic to the idea of God, *theos*. The New Atheist literature did not include Him as central to their theology. Rejecting the existence of God, then necessarily viewed Christ as superfluous to it. Not persuaded that man has a soul, they had no reason to hold Christ as someone essential to the idea of God. From time to time, Christian theists would mention his Name and purpose --- but in fact they understood neither; and, of course, the refutation always fell on the idea of "evidence for His Divinity," usually scientific evidence. Thy have no understanding of man's redemption; indeed, no concern. Sin and death seem to have another meaning for them and, to be sure, they seemed not to recognize that Christ was the Incarnate God who became a man that man might become divine.

Why do Richard Dawkins the late Christopher Hitchens, Daniel Bennet and Sam Harris propose a science which denies the existence of *God* ---- even when they know that the most famous scientists in the history of the West were theists and proponents of ot the Christian religion? Francis Thompson has an answer.

> *I fled Him, down thee nights and down the days;*
> *I fled Him, down the arches of the years;*
> *fled him down the labyrinthine ways*
> *Of my own mind; and the mist of tears*
> *I hid from Him, and under running laughter;*
> *Up vistead hopes I sped;*
> *And shot percipiatated;*
> *Adown Titanic gloom of chasmed fears*
> *From those strong Feet that followed, followed after.*
> *And with unhurring chase and unpetured pace,*
> *Deliberate speed, majestic instancy*
> *They beat --- and a Voice beat*
> *More instant than the feet*
> *All thing betray thee who betrayest hm.*

One can grasp these words in the language of Christopher Hictchens who replied to the question, "What is meaningful to you?" and he replied, "debatin' and fornicatin.'" He, as the others spoke of "the Jesus myth" (a man about which they knew very little) in order to protect their theories and their way of life. They are indifferent to the revelations of history.

With the theists, there is another answer, especially with their view of the God they espouse. It might be different if they ignored Augustine and Aquinas and the God whom they reconstructed with the philosophy of Aristotle and Platonism. They conceived God as defined by His Simplicity when His multiplicity provides a better picture of Him, that is, the Trinity and the distinction between His Essense and His Energies (Operations). Without this conception, there are a number of theological problems that could be avoided. For example, an "active Essence" which requires the creation to be necessary; or, even worse divine behavior which leads to pantheism. In any case, the Western God is the product of philosophy. If nothing else the You Tube debates confirm this accusation.

Furthermore, the arguments for the Existence of God are burdened, as any other aspect of philosophy, with the problems of epistemology. To repeat, reason can neither prove nor disprove the Existence of God, especially the true God. The New Atheists had been warned about their failure to demonstrate their position, but they seem to be disinterested in the warning and so the theory of knowledge continues to haunt their ambition. If only they believed that man was made in the "image of God" which is defiled by mortal turpitude and intellectual pride.

The New Atheists have no persuasive answer to the idea that if there is no God, everything is permissible, as Dostoyevsky exclaimed. Man can construct his own morality is the atheist response. Clearly, such a declaration is futile, because there are numerous ethical good and evil, we are condemned to relativism. Of course, someone may develop a theory of morality which he hopes to impose on the human race. But as the culture changes so does the morality that prevails at the moment. Also, there is the question of *theoretical certainty.* Without the true God, there is none. The history of modern philosophy and its purpose, nothing has been achieved. Whether empiricism or idealism, the establishment of theoretical certain has never been achieved. And for that matter, neither do the physical sciences establish it. What is true today may be compromised or lost tomorrow and that includes Darwinism.

Without the true God, there is neither ethical nor metaphysical certainty. The fault of both the theists and atheist in their You Tuble debates. The former has failed to equate the true God with the Trinity which comes by revelation not speculation.

CHAPTER VI

CONCLUSION

We must follow the evidence where it leads.
—Antony Flew

The New Atheist came to their position with a host of assumptions wholly subsumed under occidental categories, including a philosophy whose antecedents ironically originated in the so-called Dark Ages, an era profoundly religious and, therefore, a time of particular derision by modernity. Yet no one has confessed its indebtedness to that period better than Alfred North Whitehead (1861–1947) in his jewel, *Science and the Modern World* (1925). The first chapter outlines the inherited medieval principles without which there could be no science.

To start, he discusses "the widespread conviction in the Order of things" wrought by the laws of nature. The Scholastics had no reason to question whether those laws are immutable and universal inasmuch as they were part of a created and rational order. Here is the "greatest contribution of medievalism to the formation of the scientific movement, I mean the inexpugnable belief that every detailed occurrence can be correlated with its antecedent in a perfectly definite manner, exemplifying general principles." Moreover, if science is not to decay into a medley of ad hoc hypotheses, it must become philosophical and, consequently, undertake to criticize its own foundations. But the New Atheists may be aware that such criticism would lead them to the unwanted conclusion that they are indebted to medieval thought, that is, the Christian heritage of the West.

New Atheists could not maintain their position if compelled to confess that the idea of an intelligible nature was interpreted by the human mind, an idea delivered to them by a religious cosmology. Of course, they emasculated Scholastic metaphysics. In a word, New Atheism is a contradiction. Even worse, to seek justification philosophically for their atheism would oblige them to concede that atheism rests on religious (Christian) premises, that is, cosmological design and man as the image of God, rational man. So they turn to science and away from philosophy, but even here, they hide from themselves the truth that even science requires philosophical principles most evident in cosmology and anthropology. The New Atheists think of themselves as adherents of the West's science but deceive themselves when they vehemently deny their debt to religion and philosophy.

If they argue there is no personal God but nevertheless a rational order and a rational man, to what may the New Atheists turn to justify their faith but philosophy to show that the reason and science on which they depend are rightly defined and are, in fact, compatible. The harmony must exclude all arbitrariness. Above all, it is "enlightened" self-knowledge that discovers scientific truth (any truth) and reality itself. Here is where the Middle Ages and modernity, especially atheism clearly, part. The Schoolmen believed that man is the image of God and that this principle allows him to think accurately and to touch objective reality, to confidently interpret the cosmos as it presents itself to the intellect. Modernity, having knocked man from his special place in the universe, has reduced him to a limb on the evolutionary or phylogenetic tree (a little higher than apes). Yet his rational powers are assumed to be trustworthy, now without a divine guarantee. He is like everything else the product of matter and energy. He is no longer "a little lower than the angels" but merely a biological specimen.

From the biblical perspective, the "carnal" or "natural man's" reason is darkened and the range of his reason highly flawed with a limited range. His freedom of the will is diminished albeit not in "bondage" as Luther declared.

Man's *imago Dei* was not lost entirely with Adam's fall. God's grace is available to him even now, not so with the scientifically oriented New Atheists. He must inconspicuously turn to a recondite "faith," a faith in science with contempt for religion, "the opiate of the people" as Marx said, an addiction from which Dawkins, Hitchens, etc., hoped to free the human race. Who bears the truth? Reason cannot tell us. Even if it could, man's passions would frustrate his discourse. At best, right and wrong, true and false are concocted by and for the self. But there is no certainty in mere subjectivity.

Most theists turn to God for the origin of his beliefs, a divine and existential source that the heart and intellect of man experiences in numerous ways. If we can believe what the world had known for two millennia, at one time with vigor and comfort, we have our answer: the person of Jesus Christ, the Messiah, the only religious leader in the history of the world who claimed to be God himself, not a god, an angel, an ambassador, or a preacher; but the Creator of the cosmos had come among us. In his famous 1842 Berlin lectures, Friedrich Schelling jeered at the Christian doctrine of the Incarnation, saying that the Hindus claim to have experienced countless incarnations. To be sure, but they were not the absolute himself.

If only for this Man, Jesus, Christianity demands special attention. The question must be settled whether Christ was God or madman. This is a challenge that C. S. Lewis has given us. It may be argued that fundamental to this challenge is a book that for the last 250 years has come under brutal scrutiny. But its critics themselves are not free from incredulity. Let them be sardonic, but there is another powerful witness to the claims of Christ's divinity. I refer to the Church. Israel, new and old, whose sons wrote this most remarkable book, the Bible. Her testimony and existence cannot be contested. She is a historical community of believers—the prophets, Evangelists, apostles, Fathers, and all the decades and centuries of man who have linked their destiny to her. She is not a "movement" but a "great multitude of witnesses" (Heb. 12:1), some of whom foretold the redemption of Christ and some who were eyewitnesses to it. The Church has given unconditional and unaltered testimony to that history for two millennia.

Let there be no mistake. Both the Fathers and the Augustinian-Thomist tradition have provided ample evidence to the Christian revelation. These theologians are not college professors but claim to be members of the Church who in their search for spiritual perfection have met the truth through that pious quest. Traditionally, theologians have been monks, for it is they who have the time and opportunity to shed their passions that are the greatest impediment to the knowledge of the holy. What they contemplate are spiritual things that God has made accessible to those "who are purified in soul and body; or, at least, being purified" as St. Gregory the Theologian observed, things and thoughts reached by a special knowledge *(gnosis)*.

Therefore, theology is not an intellectual exercise; it is not a science. It is forbidden to the impious; it requires divine "enlightenment." "Where there is purification, there is illumination," writes St. Symeon the New Theologian (*Disc.* XII, 2). Finally, the object of his mission cannot be uncovered without grace. Let us not forget that the divine truth, including the doctrine of the Church, is therapy for the soul; it heals the heart and reason and receives the gift of special knowledge. So it is that the Church ordains that her children embrace her teachings. Here too is the key to the Scriptures, which, incidentally, do not speak to everyone. No wonder too why the New Atheists have no access to the spiritual world or sympathize with those who seek it.

Under these circumstances, what can theology mean to the atheist? — something to investigate, something to defend, something to oppose. They came to this view of theology from the Western intellectual tradition.

Ordinarily, it is a product of reason. That is how the Four Horsemen came to their theology. It is not taken seriously, not as a truth. At the same time, they bewilder religionists with mockery while showing ostensible contradictions in the Bible. Obviously, it is not a science, lacking "facts" or "evidence" at any level of inquiry.

How haughty then is the late Victor Stenger in his wild braggadocio that the New Atheists (and surely himself) have disproved the existence of God "beyond all reasonable doubt." His declamation is pure nonsense if only because he has provided no epistemological validation for it. The New Atheists have yet to determine the extent of man's rational powers. It is time for them to confess what is behind their atheism.

Moreover, because the New Atheists despise anything supernatural, they have also trivialized evil or, to use the words of Simone de Beauvoir, in their biblical exegesis, it has become "sheer banality." They are blind to the truth that there is no sharp line between good and evil. There is no sin without absolute moral standards. There is only appetite and enthusiasm. It is worth mentioning the great flaw in relativism: either it is itself relative or it is an absolute. The Four Horsemen seem unable to handle this simple truth, or do they understand that relativism is not limited to ethics? In fact, it is applicable to all forms of knowledge, to science itself. Its physical principles and postulates have not been proven to be absolute, and its discoveries lack the theoretical certainty necessary for credibility.

The New Atheists need their disbelief. They fall back on the feeble authority of reason and science so as to present themselves as "reasonable men" vis-à-vis the mindless superstition of Christians. They enjoy the taunt that God, as he is presented by religion, is both malicious and superfluous. As if to take the weapon out of the theist's fist, they proclaim that science has exploded the argument that "something cannot come from nothing." Perhaps something may spring from "no-thing" (*me on*) but not from "absolutely nothing" (*ouk on*) as Nicholas Berdyaev observed. But neither proposition precludes the need for a supernatural designer. In any case, both explanations of "nothing" are relevant to the scientific experience.

Such ideas are not found in New Atheist's literature largely because of their contempt or fear of philosophy. They show no familiarity with the development of philosophy in modern times. Perhaps for obvious reasons, they are ignorant of religious philosophers (such as Yannaras, Plantinga, Gilson, Buber, Schaeffer, etc.). Perhaps philosophy could have taught the New Atheists some humility. From

THE NEW ATHEISTS

whatever and from whomever secular knowledge may come, there is no theoretical certainty. Everything the human race has accomplished lies under the curse of doubt. Listen to Tennyson's *Ancient Sage*:

> *Thou canst not prove the Nameless, O my son*
> *Nor canst thou prove the world thou movest in.*
> *Thou canst not prove that thou art body alone*
> *Thou canst not prove that thou art spirit alone.*
> *Nor cast thou prove that thou art both in one*
> *Thou canst not prove that thou art immortal, no*
> *Nor yet that thou art mortal, nay my son*
> *Nor cast thou prove that I who speak with thee*
> *Are not thyself in converse with thyself,*
> *For nothing worth proving can be proven*
> *Nor yet disproven, wherefore thou be wise*
> *Cleave always to the sunnier side of doubt*
> *And cleave to Faith beyond the forms of Faith*

Furthermore, what the Fathers said about the philosophies of the Greeks is equally true of New Atheists; neither can change human nature. I suppose they have read Mary Shelley's *Frankenstein*. Whatever the New Atheists thinks they can accomplish, their posturing cannot bring forth a good and ethical people. It cannot achieve that end for the same reason that they cannot find God. And this brings us to another point: the wisdom of St. Paul in his first letter to the Corinthians (which Christopher Hitchens reviled for "outraging reason"). "For Christ sent me ... to preach the gospel: not with wisdom of words, lest the cross of Christ should be made of no effect. For the preaching of the Cross is to them that perish is foolishness; but unto us which are saved, it is the power of God" (1 Cor. 1:17–19).

For it is written, "I will destroy the wisdom of the wise, and will bring to nothing the understanding of the clever" (1 Cor. 1:19). St. John Chrysostom inquires, "For what sort of philosopher, which among those who have studied logic, which of those knowing of Jewish matters, has saved us and made us know the truth? Not one. It was the fishermen's work, the whole of it" (*Comm. On 1 Corinth.* hom. 5:1). Unrepentant obscurantists, the New Atheists are constitutionally blind to "wisdom," save as they define it. They are persuaded that all religion is nonsense with nothing more foolish than the Cross. What else could they say but that the Trinity, the Incarnation, the virgin birth, the Resurrection, and the Church as superstitious nonsense? They want empirically sculptured *evidence* for such things, unwilling to concede that things spiritual come to "the pure of heart," where the Spirit cleanses "the inner man" in preparation for his encounter with the divine. To repeat, they cannot recognize that the "knowledge" of spiritual things requires "enlightenment" for a mind darkened by the passions as St. Symeon the New Theologian says of unbelievers (*Disc.* IV, 1). In other terms, Christianity is primarily a spiritual condition, not only a credo.

No doubt St. Paul spoke not only Hellenistic thinkers but also to anyone who was satisfied with their earthly state and wisdom. To them all, religion, especially those that base their faith on the supernatural, is "foolish" to self- assured savants. In other words, at the back of their hostility God and the supernatural, is sinful pride as well as a sophistry, which is the greatest obstacle to apprehension of transcendent truths. It is not difficult then to imagine the ferocity of the atheist to the exclamation that "that Christ put down Plato, not by another philosopher [& scientist] of more skill but by unlearned fisherman. "For thus," writes St. John Chrysostom, "the defeat became greater, and the victory more splendid" (*ib.*, 5:2). The Greeks and Hellenizers wanted "powerful argument" and "style" to make their case. Likewise, Dawkins, Hitchens, etc., want the same advantage despite their inferiority to the ancients. The New Atheists by their words, ideas, and fulminations have proved nothing even those very few who have dipped their toe in philosophical waters. The "wisdom" by which such men want others to live and think is dangerous and reckless.

What some have called the issue of events or the occurrences in time and place make this point very well. Mao Zedong, the Communist, the atheist, and the evolutionist, caused the death of forty to seventy million people, mainly through starvation, forced labor, and executions; and it makes him the greatest democide, the most diabolical atheist in history. The perpetrator of such "events" illustrates plainly "metaphysical rebellion" against God. It seems incredible, but China is a world without its Creator. What is in the heart of such a man? What else did Satan proclaim in John Milton's *Paradise Lost* (I, 8)?

> *And reassembling our afflicted powers*
> *Consult how we may henceforth most offend*
> *Our enemy, our own loss how repair*
> *How to overcome this dire Calamity*
> *If not, what resolution from despair?*

New Atheist thinking clings to their demonic obsession, not only to obliterate God but to replace him. One of their nineteenth-century precursors, the Left Hegelian Mikhail Bakunin said, "If God exists, then He is necessarily supreme, absolute master; and if He is master, man is a slave; if man is a slave, there can be no justice, no equality, no fraternity. Therefore, I reverse the phrase of Voltaire, if God existed, it would be necessary to abolish him" (*Selected Writings*, New York, 1973, p. 125).

We see it now. His absence, his silence, has meant nothing but the loss of reason, the mad struggle for power; the human race has fallen into religious apostasy and political anarchy, which has necessitated the rule of tyrants, usually left-wing dictators, and the apotheosis of the state. In the simplest terms, the New Atheists have not located God because they do not want him. In truth, by their intellectual pomposity and self-satisfaction, they are unworthy of him. Listen once more to St. Paul, "But the natural (carnal) man receives not the things of the Spirit of God: for they are foolishness to him: neither can he know them, because they are spiritually discerned. But he that is spiritual judges all things, yet himself is judged by none" (1 Cor. 2:14–15). The Four Horsemen and all those like them have no understanding of human nature or the means to renovate it.

The New Atheists generally assume that human nature is free — Sam Harris notwithstanding. Such a position promises only relativism. Of course, that puts their atheism into doubt. In other words, without God and His Church, there is no knowledge of good and evil, right and wrong and, in the words of Dostoyevsky, "everything is permissible." Also, civilization will be characterized by apostasy and anarchy. The New Atheists promises the world a destiny of universal madness.

BIBLIOGRAPHY

Aiken, H.D., ed., *The Age of Ideology: The 19th Century Philosophers*. New York, 1956.

Angeles, P., ed. *Critiques of god: a Major statement of the Case Against Belief in God*. Buffalo (NY), 1976

Aulen, G., *Christos Victor: A Historical Study of the Three Main Types of the Idea of the Atonement*. Trans. by A.G. Herbert, New York, 1969.

Azkoul, M., *God of Our Fathers, Gods of the West: The Patristic Tradition and the New Polytheism*. Baltimore, 2009.

——-*Ye Are Gods: Salvation According to the Latin Fathers*. Dewdney, B.C. 2002.

Barth, K., *Protestant Theologians of The 19th Century: Background and History*. Trans. by B. Cozens. Grand Rapids (Mi), 2001

Barzun, J., *Darwin, Marx, Wagner: Critique of a Heritage*, New York, 1950 Baum, R.F., *Doctors of Modernity: Darwin, Marx & Freud*. Peru (Ill.), 1988.

Berdyaev, N., *The Destiny of Man*. Trans. by N.A. Duddington. London, 1954.

Bergson, H., *Creative Evolution*. Trans. A Mitchell. Mineola, NY, 1998

Berlinski, D., *The Devil's Delusion: Atheism and Its Scientific Pretensions*. New York, 2009

Burtt, E.A., ed., *The English Philosophers From Bacon to Mill*. New York, 1939.

—— *The Metaphysical Foundations of Modern Science*. New York, 2003.

Camus, A., *The Rebel: An Essay on Man in Revolt*. Trans. by A. Bower. N.Y., 1956

Casserly, J.V.M., *The Death of Man*. New York, 1967.

Cavarnos, C., *Byzantine Thought and Art*. Belmont (Mass.), 1968.

Chadwick, O., *The Secularization of the European Mind in the 19th Century*. Cambridge (Eng.), 1925

Chesterton, G.K., *The Everlasting Man*. London, 2011.

Coley, K., *The Meaning of Nietzsche's Death of God*. 11.4.08 (Internet).

Copan, P., *Is God a Moral Monster? Making Sense of the Old Testament God*. Grand Rapids (Mi), 2011.

—"Is Yahweh a Moral Monster: The New Atheists and the Old Testament: A Brief Review, ""*Philosophia Christi* X1. www/Epsociety.org/library/article.asp? pid=45.

Copleston, F.A;., *A History of Philosophy* (8 vols.). Garden City (NY), 1962- 1965).

Danielou., J., *The Bible and the Liturgy*. Trans. by Committee of Liturgical Studies. Notre Dame (Ind.), 1956.

Davies., P., *The Mind of God: The Scientific Basis for a Rational World*. New York, 1992

Dawkins, R., *The God Delusion*. New York, 2006.

—— *The Selfish Gene*. Oxford, 2006.

DeLubac, H., *The Drama of Atheist Humanism*. Trans. by E.M. Riley. New York, 1963.

Dennett, D.C., *Breaking the Spell: Religion as a Natural Phenomenon*. London, 2006.

—— *Darwin's Dangerous Idea: Evolution and the Meaning of Life*. New York, 1995.

Dostoyevsky, F., *The Brothers Karamazov*. Trans. by C. Garnett. New York. 1955.

—— *The Possessed (The Devils)*. Trans. by C. Garnett. New York, 2009.

Eagleton, T., *Reason, Faith and Revolution on the God Debate*. New York/London, 2009;

Fabio, C., *God in Exile: Modern Atheism*. Westminster (NY), 1968.

Feuerbach, L., *The Essence of Christianity*. Trans. by G. Eliot. Introduction by K. Barth with Foreword by H.R. Niehbuhr. New York, 1957.

Flew, A., *God and Philosophy*. New York, 2005.

—— *An Introduction to Philosophy of Ideas and Arguments from Plato to Popper*. New York, 1989.

—— *There is a God: How the World's Most Notorious Atheist Changed His Mind*. Introduction by R.A. Varghese. New York, 2007.

—— *The God Delusion by the Atheist Writer Richard Dawkins* (Internet)

Florovsky, G., "St Gregory Palamas and the Tradition of the Fathers," *The Greek Orthodox Theological Review* V, 2 (1959-1960), 119-131.

—— "Die Krise des Deutschen Idealismus (II): Die Krise des Idealismus als die Krise der Reformation. Ub. V. E. Luther. *Orient und Occident* (heft XII0, 1932, 2-12.

Freud, S., *The Future of an Illusion*. New York, 2011.

—— *Moses and Monotheism*. New York, 1967.

—— *Civilizations and Its Discontents*. New York, 2011.

Goethe, J. W., *Truth and Poetry: From My Own Life* (2 vols.). Trans. by P. Godwin. New York, 1855.

Gould, S., *Rock of Ages*. New York, 1999.

Hahn, S. & Wiker, B., *Answering the New Atheism: Dismantling Dawkins Against God*. Steubenville (Oh.), 2008.

Harris, S., *The End of Faith: Religion, Terror and the Future of Reason.* New York, 2004.

— *Ten Myths — and 10 Truths — About Atheism* (The Los Angeles Times 24 December 2006).

Hart, D.B., *Atheist Delusions: The Christian Revolution and Its Fashionable Enemies.* New Haven/London, 2009

Hawking, S., *A Brief History of Time.* New York, 1996

Hegel, G. W., *Early Theological Writings.* Trans. by T. Knox with And Introduction by R. Kroner. Chicago, 1948.

— *The Philosophy of Hegel.* Trans.& ed. by C.J., Friedrichs. New York, 1953.

Heidegger, M., *Was ist Das-die Philosophie?* London, 1958.

Hitchens, C., *God is Not Great: How Religion Poisons Everything.* London, 2007

— *The Portable Atheist: Essential Readings for the Non-Believer.* New York, 2009.

Hitchens, P., *The Rage Against God: How Atheism Led Me to Faith.* Grand Rapids (Mi), 2010.

Hollingsdale, R.J., *Nietzsche: the Man and His Philosophy.* Cambridge (Eng.), 1965.

Hume, D., *Dialogues Concerning Natural Religion.* Ed with Introduction Ed. by H.D. Aiken. New York, 1948.

Jastrow, R., *God and the Astronomers.* New York/London, 1978.

Jay, M., *The Dialectical Imagination: A History of the Frankfurt School And the Institute of Social Research, 1923-1950.* Berkeley (Ca). 1973.

Kalomiros, A., *Nostalgia for Paradise: Guideposts on the path to the To the true Fatherland through our Life in Christ.* Trans. by G.S. Gabriel. Ridgewood (NJ). 2006.

Kant., I., *The Critique of Pure Reason.* Trans. by J.M.D Meikeljohn. London, 1950.

Karmiris, J., "The Ecclesiology of the Three Hierarchs," *The Greek Orthodox Theological Review* VI, 2 (1960-61), 135-185.

Kaufmann, W., ed., & Trans., *The Portable Nietzsche*. New York, 1954.

— *Nietzsche: Philosopher, Psychologist, Antichrist*. New York, 1956.

Komiakov, A. S., *The Church is One*. Trans. with Introduction by Bishop Gregory Grabbe. Seattle., 1979.

Khrapovitsky, Arch. Antony, *The Dogma of Redemption*. Jordanville (NY). 1979.

LaCroix, C., *The Meaning of Atheism*. Trans with Introduction by G. Arden.

New York, 1965.

Lewis, C.S., *God in the Dock*. Grand Rapids (Mi), 1970

Lovejoy, A.O., *The Great Chain of Being: The Study of the History of an Idea*. New York, 1960

Lossky, V,. *The Mystical Theology of the Eastern Church*. Trans. by The Fellowship of St Alban and St Sergius. London, 1957.

McGrath, A., *The Twilight of Atheism: The Rise and Fall of Disbelief In the Modern World*. London, 2005.

—— and J.C. McGrath., *The Dawkins Delusion? Atheist Fundamentalism and the Denial of the Divine*. Downers Grove (Ill.), 2007

Metropolitan of Nafpaktos, *Empirical Dogmatics of the Orthodox Catholic Church According to the Spoken Teachings of Fr. John Romanides (vol. 1): Dogma-Ethics-Revelation*. Trans. by Mother Pelagia Selfe. Levadia (Greece), 2008.

Migne, J.P., ed., *Patrologiae Cursus Completus: Series Graecae* (161 vols.);

Latina (221 vols.). Paris, 1857-1866.

Miller, D., ed., *Popper Selections*. Princeton (NJ), 1985.

Mises, L. von, *Socialism: An Economic and Economic Analysis*. Trans. by J. Kahane. Indianapolis, 1981.

Nagel, T., *What Did Friedrich Nietzsche Take From Charles Darwin?* (Internet).

—— "The Fear of Religion: Review of the God Delusion." *The New Republic* (10/23/2006), 25-31.

Newell, W.L., *The Secular Magi: Marx. Freud and Nietzsche*. Cleveland (Oh), 1986.

Nicoli, A.M., *The Question of God: C.S. Lewis and Sigmund Freud: Debate: God, Love, Sex, and the Meaning of Life*. New York, 2002

Otto, R., *The Idea of the Holy*. Trans. by J.W. Harvey, Oxford, 1958.

Palmer, G.E.H., etc. Trans. and Ed, *The Philokalia* (4 vols).London, 1980

Pegis, A., ed with Intro., *Basic Writings of Thomas Aquinas* (2 vols.). New York, 1945.

Pelikan, J., *The Christian Tradition: A History of the Development of Doctrine: Spirit of Eastern Christendom (600-1700)*. Chicago, 1974.

Price, R., *The Stones Cry Out: What Archaeology Reveals About the Truth of the Bible*. Eugene (Ore), 1997

Puhalo, Archbishop Lazar, *Gehenna: The Nature of Hell According to The Orthodox Christian Church*. Dewdney, B.C., 2012.

Roberts, A. & Donaldson, ed., *The Ante-Nicene Fathers: The Writings Down to A.D. 325*.(10 vols.). Grand Rapids (<i), 1951.

Roubiczek, P., *The Misinterpretation of Man: Studies in European Man in the nineteenth Century*. London, 1949

St Isaac the Syrian, *The Ascetical Homilies*. Trans by the Holy Transfiguration Monastery. Boston, 2011.

St Simeon the New Theologian, *The Discourses*. Trans. by C.J. deCantanzaro. New York, 1980

Sagan, C., "The Demon-Haunted Science as a Candle in the Dark". New York Review of Books (Jan 9, 1997).

Schaeffer, F., *Patience with God: Faith for People who do not like Religion*. Cambridge (Mass), 2009

Schaff, P. & Wace, H., ed., *Nicene Post-Nicene Fathers* (15 vols). Grand Rapids (Mi), 1955.

Scheler, M., *The Eternal in Man*. Trans. by B. Noble. New York, 1944. Schilling, S.P., *God in the Age of Atheism*. Nashville (Tenn), 1969.

Schweitzer, A., *The Quest for the Historical Jesus*. Trans by W. Montgomery. Mineola (NY), 2005.

Shestov, L., *Athens and Jerusalem*. Trans. by B. Martin. Athens (Oh). 1966.

Smith, N.K., *A Commentary to Kant's Critique of Pure Reason*. New York, 1950.

Stenger, V.J, *The New Atheism: Taking a Stand for Science and Reason*. Amherst (NY), 2009.

Strauss, D.F., *The Life of Jesus Critically Examined*. Trans. by G. Eliot. Philadelphia, 1972.

Swinburne, R., "Response to Richard Dawkins Criticisms in *The God Delusion*" (Internet)

Tucker, R., ed., *The Marx-Engels Reader*. New York, 1972.

Tillich, P., *Perspective in 19th & 20th Century Protestant Theology*. New York, 1967.

Wilson, A.N., *God's Funeral*. New York, 1999. Watts, A., *The Way of Zen*. New York, 1985.

Whitehead, A.N., *Science and the Modern World*. New York, 1967.

Zacharias, R., *The End of Reason: A Response to the New Atheists*. Grand Rapids (Mi). 2008

— *Can Man Live without God*. Nashville (Tenn), 1994.

www.ingramcontent.com/pod-product-compliance
Ingram Content Group UK Ltd.
Pitfield, Milton Keynes, MK11 3LW, UK
UKHW022226230426
12048UKWH00016BA/1082